The Growplan Gardening Guide

Written and edited by
Brian Gibbons

With contributions from
Ray Edwards, Geoff Amos, Les Jones,
Derek Cox and other Garden News experts

David & Charles
Newton Abbot   London   North Pomfret (Vt)

garden
news

British Library Cataloguing in Publication Data

Gibbons, Brian
   The growplan gardening guide.
   1. Gardening
   I. Title
   635   SB453
   ISBN 0-7153-7697-7

Printed in Great Britain
by A. Wheaton & Co. Limited Exeter (AW)
for David & Charles (Publishers) Limited
Brunel House Newton Abbot Devon

Published in the United States of America
by David & Charles Inc
North Pomfret Vermont 05053 USA

Contents

Introduction

Although unfortunately it is no longer true that every home has a garden, every garden should be regarded as part of the home. Not just in terms of property but as an exciting extension to family life. All the occupants of a house get full benefit from the dining-room, bathroom, kitchen and bedroom, but what about the biggest room of all, the one that offers the most in the way of enjoyment and mutual fulfillment—the outdoor room?

All too often the garden is a neglected patch of grass and weeds, dismissed as a necessary evil, somewhere for the kids and pets to be turned out into, somewhere to dry the washing. Certainly it should fulfil these roles—but what a waste to leave it at that.

All the family should be encouraged to share the pleasures that the outdoor room can offer, to plan and plant, to have their own interests and responsibilities, to work

and relax, to play their part in developing its potential and to take their share of the immense satisfaction in seeing their own ideas and plants blossom into reality.

You should see the garden as an extension of the home in real terms as well as in attitude. Seen from indoors it is a series of constantly changing, three-dimensional pictures framed by the windows. Why not paint a masterpiece to enhance the room you are in? When you are in the garden what dominates the scene? The house. Make it attractive: help the plain walls to harmonise with their surroundings by adding a few hanging baskets, window boxes, flower and shrub tubs, or perhaps a climbing rose or clematis to soften the mass of brickwork. There is nothing like a patio or balcony suitably furnished with plants to link the house and garden—the indoor and outdoor rooms. Visual and personal pride apart, it makes good sense if you are an owner–occupier to increase the value of your home.

Talking of financial benefits, what about the savings you can make by growing your own vegetables and fruit? In even the tiniest garden, perhaps just a back yard, there is still room to put in a few salad crops. Three tomato plants in a growing bag up against a wall take hardly any room at all, while the space occupied by one small cold frame or three or four cloches will produce maybe a dozen spring lettuces when they are most expensive to buy and a few bunches of spring onions and radishes.

If you are fortunate enough to have a larger plot to devote to home-grown produce the possibilities are endless. Just think of being self-sufficient in terms of fresh fruit and vegetables; never having to visit the greengrocer again except for foreign fruit and nuts. This is quite possible if you keep your soil in good condition and plan carefully to have crops ready for harvesting all the year round.

The home freezer has opened up even more possibilities. Those seasonal gluts of peas and beans, and many other vegetables, need not be eaten up quickly until the family is sick of the sight of them; pop them in the freezer, and come winter you have the additional satisfaction of your own produce from the previous season steaming on the plate, fresh as the day it was picked. Past triumphs are re-lived!

What about a greenhouse or conservatory? Many new interests will unfold. Collections of cacti, succulents and tropical plants perhaps; winter-flowering plants such as cinerarias and calceolarias to bring into the house for decoration; a longer season for tomatoes and cucumbers; outdoor flowers and vegetables started off that much earlier; and, probably most important of all, most of the plants that the garden requires raised from seed and cuttings. Bearing in mind the high cost of, for instance, annual bedding plants and the large numbers required to put on a reasonable display, the saving on this item alone will soon begin to repay the cost of some sort of glass.

There are so many other aspects of gardening to delight and stimulate the family: the pleasures of rose growing . . . learning the art of flower arranging with materials gathered from your own patch . . . taking a particular interest in rockery or pond plants . . . the satisfaction of having built a walled raised bed or of laying crazy paving . . . you may even fancy exhibiting your produce and become involved with the local garden society.

Whatever your pleasure, this book, based on the weekly Growplan series in *Garden News*, is designed to help you get more from it—more success, more enjoyment, a greater understanding of the ways of nature and, above all, a greater desire to get cracking and do even better next year.

Dividing this book into separate, self-contained sections presented a problem. Gardening just isn't like that. All of the different aspects are integrated into one well-organised, smooth-running site. There is bound to be some overlapping—especially in the greenhouse. All of the contents of that section could belong under other headings—flowers, vegetables, fruit. What I have done is to place all plants, whatever they are, that are grown specifically for the greenhouse or that spend a large part of their lives under glass in that section, together with other outdoor plants that come in at certain times for propagation, etc. This is why indoor tomatoes and cucumbers, for instance, will be found in the greenhouse section while outdoor types are discussed in the vegetable section.

Happy gardening . . . .

Brian Gibbons

Planning

Keeping the family happy

When planning a garden remember what was said earlier about it being an extension of the house. Just as the home is fitted out and furnished to accommodate all the members of the family, so should those large outdoor rooms—the front and back gardens. Don't make the mistake of trying to cram in as much as possible, however. Just as a small room that is cluttered tends to look even smaller, so will it be in the garden.

Before you begin to plan your ideal garden, it would be wise to consult your husband or wife. One of you may well have preferences for particular plants or colours, or have some lifelong dream of a wishing well, pond or rockery. The other may appreciate a private, sunny corner in which to acquire a Riviera tan, a handy little herb plot or a bed of prize marrows.

What about the children? To them a garden is a playground. Any lawn or piece of open ground, however small, is fated to become, according to season, their miniature Wembley, Lords, Wimbledon or Olympic stadium. If space doesn't allow them to have a separate area, try to site greenhouses, frames and other fragile structures away from the flight path of balls, arrows and similar missiles.

Here are some other points to consider if you are to keep all of the family happy. How much space do you intend to devote to vegetables; what about fruit; will you need a shed; will you have much time to spend on gardening; are you approaching the age when you

won't feel like, or be capable of, much bending or heavy work; would you be better off planning a garden that, once established, requires a minimum of maintenance? Far better to ask and answer all of these questions now, before you start work.

Drawing the plan

Before getting your ideas down on paper you have to draw in the 'frame'—the boundary of the garden. Take the trouble to measure it accurately, because if the dimensions are wrong you'll be in trouble later when you come to mark out the real thing. Make a note of any drains, manholes, gates or variations in level. If you are re-designing an existing garden, draw in any features that are to be retained—paths, trees, shrubs, buildings, walls or hedges.

Remember to draw, with a compass as your guide, the north point—an arrow pointing north with a large N at the top. Only by knowing the aspect of your garden can you work out where the house shadows will fall, which parts will catch the sun at which time of day, which will be the south-facing, warmest walls against which to grow the more tender plants and where to position screening for protection against cold north and east winds.

The next step is to divide the still fairly empty plan into sections: a vegetable patch, rockery, lawn, play area, pool, greenhouse and so on. This will give a good indication of where paths, walls, screens and borders will fall.

If you want to make the garden appear longer than it really is, position a natural-looking part-screen of shrubs, ornamental trees or climbing plants on a trellis about two-thirds of the way down the site. A glimpse through the screen of more garden beyond always gives an impression of greater length. The space behind could be given to the vegetable or fruit patch, the shed, cold frames or anything that you don't want to be in full view.

In the main area, unless you particularly like formal, regimented gardens, try to avoid straight lines. Gentle, interesting curves for the outlines of beds, borders and lawns, and winding paths add to the air of informality. Always ensure that paths lead somewhere interesting— perhaps a sundial, pool or rustic arch.

Even if straight paths are your choice, make rounded corners rather than right angles. They are far easier to negotiate with a barrow or truck and, if bordering a lawn, mowing into the corner can be done in one sweep.

Having chosen the features that best suit you and your family, arrange them as you would furniture in a room. Aim for a pleasant balance with ample space to move about and relax and with all the best pieces where they can be seen and admired. In fact, as house and garden should be considered as a single unit, why not link the two together with a patio, balcony or walk-through conservatory. Climbing plants and hanging baskets on the exterior walls, and flower troughs and tubs help too.

Paths should always lead to something interesting—in this case down steps to a sunken rock garden

Trees: the height of elegance

Height is just as important a dimension as distance and to exploit its possibilities to the full you must include some trees. By giving some thought to the choice of trees and their position you can have a pleasant background and the rich and varied colours of their foliage and blossom, especially at times of the year when the rest of the garden looks rather bare.

Badly positioned trees or shrubs quickly become liabilities however—easy enough to plant but difficult to shift once they become established—so here are a few pointers to help you:

1 Get the right species in the right place to start with.
2 Try to visualise what small trees and shrubs will look like in ten, fifteen or even more years' time when they have grown considerably. Will they confine themselves to the space you have allowed or will they engulf their surroundings?
3 Few annual bedding plants are happy under dripping foliage, so avoid overhanging borders and beds.
4 Don't place them where they will cast shadows over places that need full sun, such as rockeries, a patio or sunbathing area.
5 Trees and shrubs make excellent windbreaks, filtering and diluting the unseen forces that can damage less sturdy plants and buildings.
6 Just as planting potentially large trees in small areas is a mistake, so is planting nothing but small, low-growing ones in a large garden. Big gardens need some big trees to give perspective and focal points.
7 When positioning trees to suit your own needs don't forget that you have some responsibility towards your neighbours as well. They won't appreciate shadow-casting, leaf-shedding, light-blocking trees right up to the boundary fence and overhanging their property.

Plants for awkward areas

Camouflaging eyesores Many favourite shrubs are ideal for covering unsightly walls, fences, dead trees and even outbuildings as well as for clothing trellises and screens. These include climbing roses, honeysuckle, clematis and ivies. Probably the best two for covering large eyesores are *Clematis montana* and *Polygonum baldschuanicum* (Russian vine). There are quite a lot of quick-growing annual climbers that will do the same job provided they are given adequate support. There are sweet peas, which also provide fragrant, long-stemmed blooms to take into the house, the climbing type of nasturtiums, ornamental gourds, *Cobaea scandens*, *Convolvulus major*, *Humulus japonicus* (annual hop), *Ipomoea rubro-coerulea* and *Mina lovata*. Free-standing trees to plant in front of eyesores include quick-growing conifers such as the Leyland cypress or the shrubby herringbone cotoneaster, *C. horizontalis*.

Banks and rough ground If left to their own devices these problem areas quickly become overgrown with weeds, so get them planted up with more desirable subjects. Ground cover plants are the answer and there are many suitable annual and perennial flowers and shrubs. On really rough ground it is advisable to get annual plants well established in pots before putting them in position.

The natural architecture of trees is essential to any garden

Here are a few possibilities: perennial aster, annual chrysanthemum, calendula, *Agrostemma gigatho, Convolvulus major* and *C. minor*, coreopsis, cornflower, *Echium plantagineum,* eschscholztia, lavatera, linaria, limnanthes, *Linum grandiflorum,* lupin, nasturtium, nigella, poppy, Virginian stock, ajuga, geranium, lamium, hypericum, polygonum, vinca and veronica. Of course a nice sunny bank would be the ideal situation on which to build a rockery.

Shady areas Not all plants rely on the sun and full light. There are a great many woodland subjects that get little sun in their natural habitat and are just the things for dark areas of the garden. Shrubs include selected rhododendrons and azaleas, bamboo, cornus, aucuba, weigela, honeysuckle, hypericum, *Mahonia aquifolium* and skimmias. Flowers to be used include hosta, saxifraga (London pride), primula, lobelia, astilbe, geranium and anemone.

Damp areas Careful selection is needed here, but among the plants that thrive with wet feet are hosta, primula, ferns, trollius, mimulus (musk), astilbe and caltha.

Exposed to winds Plants to look for here are those that will not suffer leaf scorch, be blown out of the ground or broken off. Low-growers are favourite, but taller subjects will survive if well staked and protected. Try potentilla, sedum, alyssum, geranium, dwarf conifers, heathers and stachys.

Lime or chalk soils Although your choice needs careful thought if you are in an area with this type of soil, there are still many lovely plants to serve you well. Flowers include anemone, dianthus, gypsophila, iris, alyssum, campanula, the grow-anywhere geranium, peonies, linaria, aquilegia, hypericum and prunella. Among shrubs are clematis, buddleia, forsythia, roses, prunus, veronica, syringa, philadelphus, cytisus, cistus, laburnum, viburnums and chaenomeles (quince).

Some garden plans

Piecemeal garden planning results in a confusion of ideas with no co-ordination and little purpose. In short, a mess. Even if the work is spread over several years, a master plan should be drawn up so that each separate part complements, and harmonises with, the rest. Types of gardens fall into three main categories—productive, family and luxury.

These two plans show how a garden can be planned and planted in two totally different ways.

Plan A is a design for a family garden, with a large area of rough grass at the bottom of the plot where the children can play happily without damaging the productive and ornamental areas.

Plan B is a productive garden with only a small area devoted to ornamental planting. There are three separate plots—for vegetables, salad crops and fruit.

The main flowers in this delightful bank are perennial asters

A

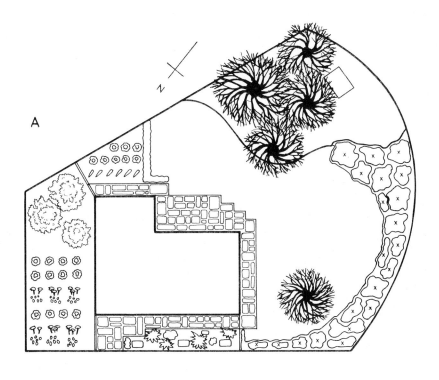

B

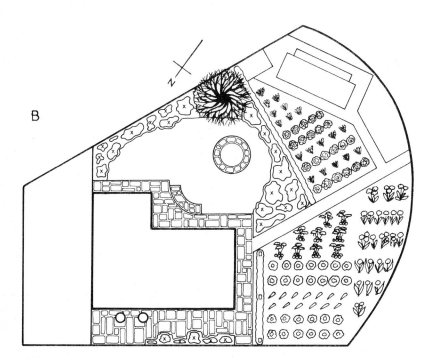

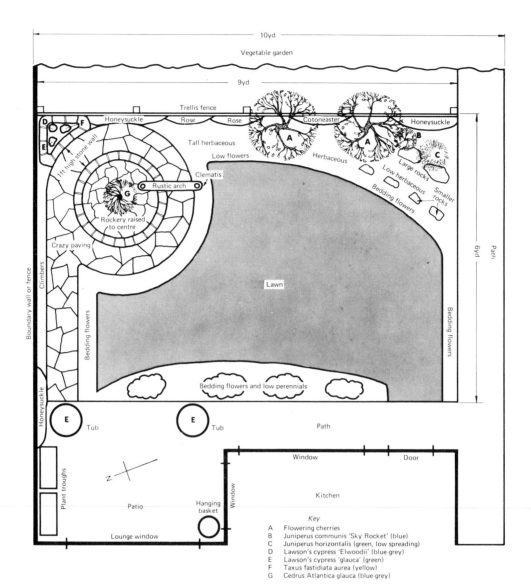

Key
A   Flowering cherries
B   Juniperus communis 'Sky Rocket' (blue)
C   Juniperus horizontalis (green, low spreading)
D   Lawson's cypress 'Elwoodii' (blue-grey)
E   Lawson's cypress 'glauca' (green)
F   Taxus fastidiata aurea (yellow)
G   Cedrus Atlantica glauca (blue-grey)

A layout for the ornamental section of a small back garden with vegetables at the rear screened by a shrub-covered trellis. The householder wanted to retain the straight path running up the right-hand side and this left a small rectangle 9yds (8.2m) wide by 6yds (5.5m) long. To escape from this restrictive shape, full use has been made of circles and curves. Other requirements were interesting views from all the house windows and sufficient lawn to take a swing, slide or paddling pool for his two young children. His wife requested the flowering cherries and areas for climbing and rock plants.

Most of the flowering shrubs have been given south or west-facing positions where they are sheltered by fences or walls from the cold winds.

The circular rockery is also in the sunniest corner and, as it is the main feature of the layout, is raised so that it can be seen from the house. Because falling leaves are a nuisance in a rockery, it is well clear of the deciduous trees. The rest of the trees are evergreen conifers of various sizes, shapes and colours to give year-round interest. Apart from trees and climbers, height is provided by a rustic arch along which clematis will be trained. Provision is also made for herbaceous perennial and annual bedding flowers.

The centre of the patio will be occupied by a garden table and chairs during the warm months and full use is made of plant containers to bring colour on to the paving and to link the house and garden.

Preparation

Everything depends on the soil

Of all the raw materials at our disposal the most important by far is the soil itself—after all this is the medium in which our plants will grow and that will, directly or indirectly, provide most of their requirement of nutrients and moisture. Get the soil right and you are more than halfway towards successful gardening.

Structurally there are four main ingredients—clay, chalk, sand and humus (decomposed organic matter). Usually there is too much of one or other of the first three and not enough of the fourth. It is simple enough to determine from the texture and colour which ingredient you have in excess and, although the treatments may well take several years and a lot of work, you will never get the best from your garden without them. When the balance between all four is perfect you have loam, which is fertile, easy to cultivate, free-draining and open.

Carry out your own chemical test by means of one of the simple do-it-yourself analysis kits that are readily available. Some give merely the lime/acid balance or pH, while the slightly more expensive ones will also tell you if there is a deficiency in any of the essential nutrients—nitrogen, phosphorus and potash.

Types of soil

There are six basic types likely to be encountered in Britain—sandy, chalky, gravel, clay, peaty and loamy. To improve their texture the first four all require the addition of plenty of humus—organic matter such as garden compost, farmyard manure, peat, pulverised bark or spent hops—either to help hold water and plant food close to the roots instead of letting it soak straight through out of reach, or in a clay soil to break up the sticky

mass, making it easier to work, allowing in air and at the same time releasing the surprisingly high proportion of plant foods locked up within. In fact well-cultivated clay is one of the most fertile soils.

The other two types are naturally the most rewarding and pleasant to work without much preparatory labour. The loams, which can have a slight tendency towards being sandy, clay or peaty without affecting the ideal balance too much, are capable of growing a wide range of plants. Peaty soils, such as you find in fen or moorland areas, can be warm, fertile and friable, but they may be on the acid side and need regular dressings of lime.

All about pH The pH of a soil is a figure arrived at by chemical testing which accurately defines the degree of acidity or alkalinity (lime). At the top of the scale, pH $7\frac{1}{2}$ is very limy and then by $\frac{3}{4}$ degrees it goes down to pH $4\frac{1}{2}$, which is acid. In practice then, the range covers five types of soil:

A pH $7\frac{1}{2}$ Limy
B pH $6\frac{3}{4}$ About right for many plants
C pH 6 Below neutral, needs lime
D pH $5\frac{1}{4}$ Needs lime badly
E pH $4\frac{1}{2}$ Acid.

Soils C, D and E are suitable for lime-hating plants. To change a soil of one of these types to the one immediately above or below it, note the following: To make it one step more alkaline (limy) add 5lb (2.25kg) of ground limestone to every 100sq ft (9.3sq m). To make it one step more acid, add 30–40lb (13.6–18kg) of peat or $\frac{1}{2}$cwt (25kg) of manure or 1cwt (50kg) of garden compost to every 100sq ft (9.3sq m).

Alternatively, add $1\frac{1}{2}$lb (680gm) of sulphate of ammonia, aluminium sulphate or sulphur.

Does lime content matter? How much does it matter to the plants whether the soil they are in contains lime or not? Most plants are accommodating and will manage in all kinds of soil, but a few things we grow have strong dislikes. Some can't stand lime at any price, others can't stand an acid soil. Here is an easy-reference table, using the A-E coding to show which soils suit some ordinary garden plants.

Scillas	A–B	Lupin	C–D
Snowdrop	A–B	Maranta	C–D
Sweet peas	A–B	Monstera	C–D
Sweet William	A–B	Philodendron	C–D
Verbena	A–B	Phlox	C–D
Wisteria	A–B	Rubber plant	C–D
Yucca	A–B	Billbergia	C–E
Fuchsia	C	Heather	C–E
Gloxinia	C	Cacti	D
Grevillea	C	Camellia	D
Hoya	C	Laurel	D
Impatiens	C	Lily-of-the-valley	D
Pansy	C	Aspidistra	D–E
Primrose	C	Azalea	D–E
Shrimp plant	C	Columnea	D–E
Cissus	C–D	Holly	D–E
Dogwood	C–D	Orchids	D–E
Gardenia	C–D	Rhododendron	D–E

Testing for lime

1 When using the Sudbury lime-testing kit, take a sample from about 2–3in (5–7cm) below the surface and put the samples into a clean polythene bag. Transfer them into clean containers and allow them to dry naturally—not over direct heat.

Fruit and vegetables

Artichoke (Jerusalem)	A–B	Blackberries	C–D
Asparagus	A–B	Chicory	C–D
Leek	A–B	Gooseberries	C–D
Mushrooms	A–B	Potatoes	C–D
Plums	A–B	Strawberries	C–D
Apples	C–D	Blueberries	D–E
		Cranberries	D–E

Flowers, shrubs and houseplants

Ageratum	A–B	Ivy	A–B
Berberis	A–B	Lilies	A–B
Canna	A–B	Morning glory	A–B
Daphne	A–B	Myrtle	A–B
Eucalyptus	A–B	Oxalis	A–B
Forget-me-not	A–B	Philadelphus	A–B
Forsythia	A–B	Petunia	A–B
Geranium	A–B	Pinks	A–B
Honeysuckle	A–B	Poppies	A–B

2 Quarter-fill the test tube with finely powdered soil from the samples and add the required amount of reagent. Cork the tube, shake well and allow the mixture to settle. A comparison of colours with the chart will determine pH.

When the ground needs liming, mark off and treat a square metre at a time to ensure that you apply the correct dosage

Manuring and composting

Contrary to what many people think, it is not as a fertiliser that manures or garden composts are most valuable, although they help of course. The composition of both is so variable that you can never be quite certain what proportions of the basic nutrient elements you are putting in. Anyway there is unlikely to be sufficient quantity of nutrient and a supplementary dressing of a balanced fertiliser is strongly recommended.

Manures and composts help to enrich the ground, of course, but their main function is to improve its structure. But if the ground is naturally short of goodness, as most will be if previously cropped, something else will be needed. With a general fertiliser that has the ideal balance raked into the surface, well-composted or manured ground will grow almost anything.

Compost is free Good farmyard manure is often difficult to come by these days, but most gardens can support a compost heap. Quite simply, compost consists of organic waste materials from garden or house that have been encouraged to decompose into a dark, crumbly, soil-like matter rich in humus. Waste plant tops, roots, etc, from an allotment or vegetable patch are never enough on their own to re-treat the same area of ground properly. It's better to use what you have generously in the places you consider most important than to spread it about thinly.

On the other hand, if you have a fair supply of lawn mowings and leaves, plus prunings, discarded plants, dead flowers and other waste from the ornamental garden, as well as peelings and organic refuse from the kitchen, and compost all this intelligently, you might have enough to keep an average vegetable garden in good trim, and it will go even further in the flower garden. Anything that has once lived will produce compost. This can include shredded and soaked newspapers, comics, books and even old clothes and carpets if they are not made of nylon or other man-made materials.

A container of some sort is needed to make compost properly and to keep it in a tidy heap. Better still, have two containers, one for filling with new material, one for providing compost ready for use. Try to keep the ingredients well mixed and add any possible animal manure,

Before: vegetable and fruit peelings are emptied into a compost container

After: well-rotted compost is collected from the container

A home-made compost container

Rotting down autumn leaves by covering them with polythene

such as from pets or poultry, or failing this one of the proprietary accelerators to speed up the rotting and composting process. Three requirements are needed for quick and thorough decomposition—warmth, water (but not too much) and air. Once the bacteria get to work the heap or binful will generate its own heat and should be ready for use in two to three months in summer or up to six months in winter.

Other types of composts For those not able to obtain farmyard manure or make compost there are various processed materials available, generally in clean polythene bags. They range from treated sewage and dustbin refuse composted into an acceptable peat-like mixture, through peat-plus fertilisers, to actual concentrated farmyard manures. These are generally complete, needing no additives, but rather expensive to scatter around *ad lib* all over the garden and are better used under or around particular areas, crops or individual plants.

Peat on its own, spent mushroom compost or pulverised tree bark also make good substitutes, but like garden compost they are short of nutrients and a balanced fertiliser should be raked in.

Digging

Single-spit digging, that is turning the top soil over to the depth of a spade or fork, is enough to grow plants adequately for years on end, providing manure or humus and fertiliser are regularly added. But the ground and the plants can be improved by occasional deeper digging. Once in five or six years it should be the aim to double-dig at least a portion of any patch. On new ground it will pay in most cases to double-dig it all in the first

A good clear trench is essential for double digging. After one spit has been dug out, the bottom of the trench is broken up with a fork

14

year. It is not as formidable a job as it sounds: it just takes twice as long as ordinary digging.

It consists of breaking up the second spit down. This hard layer develops in all gardens, but particularly where the soil is heavy. Opening it up improves aeration and drainage and gives much better root growth. It is a place, too, where all kinds of weeds and rubbish that naturally occur in a neglected garden can be buried.

The first step is to mark out a 2ft (60cm) wide strip across the patch. Then dig all the soil out to a spade depth, clearing it to a level bottom, and wheel the displaced soil to where you are going to finish. Next, get in the trench and turn the bottom over with a fork, digging in all the weeds and waste, manure or compost that you can spare. Then, turn to the next 2ft (60cm) wide strip. Skim all the rough grass, etc, off the top and put it on top of the digging you have just done. Then dig the top spit over on top of it. This, when properly done, leaves another trench to get into and break up as the first.

Fertilisers

Plants gradually use up the nutrients in soil, so the purpose of fertilisers, either organic or inorganic, is to replace them and maintain a general balance of fertility. The required balance is made up of the three major nutrients—nitrogen, phosphorus and potash—plus a range of minor and micro-nutrients needed in minute quantities. Basically, nitrogen encourages leaf and stem growth, phosphorus strengthens root development, while potash is important for the formation of flowers and fruit and for ripening.

Fertilisers are widely available in pre-mixed forms, usually containing all the major nutrients and sometimes with the minor ones added to give a complete food. You can also make up your own mixtures. There are different fertilisers for different seasons, as well as ones for particular types of plants—tomatoes, roses, chrysanths, shrubs, etc. Individual or 'straight' fertilisers are still widely used, especially for vegetables or fruit. They may contain one or more nutrients, but should be used with care to prevent excess symptoms or scalding.

Fertilisers are sold either dry in granule, dust or crystal form, or in concentrated solutions. It is vital to read the manufacturer's instructions about rates of application or dilution. Where powdery forms are also recommended as liquid feed, it may help to mix the required amount with a little water to form a thick slurry before adding the remaining water.

Where powerful chemical 'straights' are employed they should be either watered on to the soil (taking care not to get any on the plants), or applied to moist soil.

Liquid feeding can be applied either direct to the foliage for almost immediate effect, or to the surrounding soil.

On no account apply it to pots where the compost is dry, otherwise the roots are bound to be scalded. Foliar feeding is best if a plant lacks a good root system.

Organic fertilisers

Bonemeal Phosphate-rich and slow-acting—the finer the powder the more rapid the availability to plants.

Raking a general balanced fertiliser into the soil surface just before sowing or planting is standard practice with many gardeners

Foliar feeds should be applied as a fine spray

Steamed bone flour is similar, but considered less of a health risk.

Dried blood   Usually supplied as a dry powder and containing fair quantities of readily available nitrogen. Apply dry to soil at 2oz per sq yd (60gm per sq m) or dilute in water—1oz per gallon (25gm per 4 litres).

Fishmeal   Contains quantities of all major nutrients, but normally supplied with additions of other fertilisers to give a more balanced diet.

Hoof and horn   Apply outside at 2oz per sq yd (60gm per sq m) for steady release of nitrogen.

Seaweed concentrate   Ideal for foliar feeding or where minor nutrients may be lacking. Apply as instructions.

Soot   Care must be taken if domestic soot is used as it is caustic when fresh (ideal for repelling slugs). Store dry for four months, then apply any time at the rate of 6oz per sq yd (180mg per sq m). Contains good amounts of nitrogen.

Wood ash   Nutrient value varies with type of wood, but high in potash. Store dry or nutrient will be leached out; apply up to 8oz per sq yd (240gm per sq m).

Inorganic fertilisers

Basic slag   Slow-acting type supplying phosphate and some lime in varying amounts. Apply autumn and winter after digging at the rate of 4–8oz per sq yd (120–240g per sq m).

Muriate of potash   Readily soluble form of pure potash, but tends to scorch roots if not used sparingly. Apply in winter $\frac{1}{2}$–1oz per sq yd (15–30gm per sq m).

Nitrate of soda   Soluble nitrogen fertiliser for spring and summer application (ideal for boosting green crops) but take care not to touch foliage or mix with superphosphate. Tends to make clay soil more sticky. Apply $\frac{1}{2}$–1oz per sq yd (15–30gm per sq m) or, in solution, $\frac{1}{4}$–$\frac{1}{2}$oz per gallon of water (6–12gm per 4 litres).

Nitro-chalk   Quick-acting proprietary granular type supplying nitrogen and lime. Good for acid soils. Apply 1oz per sq yd (30gm per sq m).

Sulphate of ammonia   Best used spring or early summer $\frac{1}{2}$–1oz per sq yd (15–30gm per sq m). Similar in action to nitrate of soda but safer to use. Don't mix with lime.

Sulphate of potash   Best form of potash for general use as it's not caustic and is fairly quick-acting. Use at any time, $\frac{1}{2}$–1oz per sq yd (15–30gm per sq m).

Superphosphate   Ideal where phosphates are needed quickly, particularly in spring or summer. Apply 1–3oz per sq yd (30–90gm per sq m). Often known as superphosphate of lime, but contains no free lime, so can be used for lime-hating plants too.

Permanent standing plants such as fruit bushes are greatly helped by a dressing of fertiliser over their root area. Two or more ounces in early spring are generally enough for an ordinary fruit bush

Opposite

Above Even a tiny garden benefits from a small pool such as this one, which brings a patch of reflected sky down to ground level. A nice planting of polyanthus completes the picture. *Below* This large pool has been used to introduce aquatic and marginal plants into the garden. In the foreground are graceful candelabra primulas, which do best in wet, boggy soil, such as along the banks of pools and streams, while the floating leaves and cool-looking flowers of the water lily are always favourite.

Mix your own general fertiliser

If a general garden fertiliser is required for pre-sowing or planting, use the following: 5 parts sulphate of ammonia, 7 parts superphosphate, 2 parts sulphate of potash and 1 part steamed bone flour (all parts by weight). Apply this mixture 3–5oz per sq yd (90–150gm per sq m) or 1–2oz per gallon of water (25–50gm per 4 litres) a week or so before sowing or planting, then at intervals during the growing season to vigorous crops.

Changing an existing layout

It is often easier, once you have cleared away the builders' rubble, to start off a new garden from scratch. Harder work maybe, but at least it's easier to decide what ought to go where. It is rare to move into an existing house and find that the previous occupier has arranged his garden exactly as you would like it to be.

Unless they are hopelessly in the wrong place large trees and shrubs must be regarded as permanent features and any new plans based around them. The same may apply to any outbuildings, walls, etc.

Smaller trees and shrubs—roses for instance—that are in the wrong place can often be moved. If their new sites are not yet ready they can be given a temporary refuge. Find a sheltered spot that is not involved in the changes and, any time during the dormant period between October and March, dig them out, damaging the roots as little as possible, and heel them in there.

Whatever time of year you take up residence some plants will not be showing. There may be the roots of herbaceous plants that have finished flowering and been cut down to ground level, or many bulbs, corms or tubers lying dormant in the soil. The first you will know of them is when you begin turning them up when digging, often causing great damage. The outgoing occupier might take you round pointing out where various plants are hidden, but it may be better to shelve replanning schemes for one whole year, until you have seen just what surprises spring up and can mark them.

What about if the lawn needs to be moved too? If the turf is in reasonable condition it can be cut and lifted, taking great care to maintain an even thickness, and relaid in its new position. But more about laying a lawn in a later chapter (see page 149). If the existing turf is poor, either kill it off with a weedkiller—not one that will have a long-term effect on the soil—or roughly cut

The most widely used fertiliser for mixing with potting soils is John Innes base, which can be bought ready made. To make J.I.No.1 add 4oz (112g) to each bushel (36.4 l) of the soil, peat and sand mixture. J.I.No.2 takes 8oz (224g) and J.I.No.3 takes 12oz (336g)

and lift it and stack it upside-down somewhere out of the way so that it can be left to rot down into splendidly rich loam.

When the features to be retained have been decided, and everything wrongly positioned has been moved, the ground undergoing change has to be cleared and cleaned. For the first occupier of a new house this is the situation with the whole of his garden.

Before even thinking about digging and planting, all large stones, bricks and general rubbish must be picked off. Some of it may come in handy later for hardcore in construction work.

Take advantage of the opportunity to make a completely clean start. Get rid of all weeds and rubbish now, while the ground is empty of plants, and save a lot of trouble later. When you get round to digging, the persistent perennials such as docks, nettles, dandelions, couch grass, brambles and convolvulus should be picked out and burned. It will be much more difficult to shift them when they grow up in the new rockery, or in the middle of clumps of herbaceous plants.

Opposite

Above Just two of the many hundreds of different sempervivums, still known affectionately as 'house leeks' because they used commonly to be seen growing on roofs of old houses. In rockeries, troughs and sink gardens they are double value plants, having delightful rosetted foliage and throwing up tall handsome flower stems. *Below* One of the most common and best-loved spring-time rockery plants is aubretia, with its masses of blue, mauve and pink flowers. Other spring flowers adding colour to this rockery are bellis daisies, pansies and alyssum.

Seed buying

When choosing flower seeds you should know the habits
and requirements of the resultant plants. On the packets
are letters that tell what you need to know: HA means
hardy annual; HHA half-hardy annual; HB hardy biennial;
and HP hardy perennial. These terms tell how the plants
grow, when they flower, at what time of year the seed
should be sown and where.

Hardy annuals are sown outside in the garden during
spring, should be thinned out but not transplanted, flower
in summer and autumn and then die.

Half-hardy annuals are sown under glass in January,
February or March, pricked out into boxes or pots, hardened off and planted out in May to flower in summer,
after which they die too.

Hardy biennials are sown outside or in seed boxes
in May, transplanted into nursery rows in July and on
into flowering positions in October. They stand the winter,
flower during the following spring and early summer and
then die.

Hardy perennials are treated in much the same way
as biennials, but make permanent plants to come up and
flower every year.

Pelleted seeds or not?   That's a decision we have to
make these days because most firms offer a range of
them. After the dry summers of 1975 and 1976 many
people were put off pellets by poor results. The trouble
was that moisture is needed to break down the surrounding clay coat. In a drought there is not enough natural

moisture about to germinate even uncoated seeds, and
those enclosed in a fairly hard coating have very little
chance.

Nevertheless for people who find it difficult to sow
sparsely enough to avoid much thinning-out and plant
wastage later, pelleted seeds are easier to handle. If the
ground at sowing and germination time is dry, you can
always first water the drills and then keep the beds moist.

Weedkillers

Although cultivated areas can be kept clean by good hus-
bandry, if ever there was a conclusive argument in favour
of using chemicals in the garden, weeds in difficult places
such as lawns and paths provide it.

What is a weed? Any plant growing in the wrong place
merits that description, although in their proper place they
may be greatly cherished. Seedlings of even such popular
flowers as *Anemone blanda* will eventually take over a
garden if not checked.

As with all plants, there are annuals such as chickweed
and groundsel, soft-stemmed herbaceous perennials like
couch grass, bindweed and ground elder, and woody perennials like brambles and ivy.

Chemical weedkillers can basically be divided into two
types—those that act through the leaves and those that
work through the roots, although some do both. Selective

leaf-acting types (hormone weedkillers) such as 2,4-D and mecoprop are the most widely used, especially to treat lawns without damaging the grass. Root-acting types usually depend for their selectivity on the rate of application.

Total, non-selective weedkillers such as sodium chlorate destroy every growth they make contact with (including trees if used over the root area) and are useful for completely clearing rough ground, their effect persisting for up to eight months. Other non-selectives like diquat and paraquat kill off only the above-ground growth, making them especially effective against annuals, and neutralise on contact with the soil.

Then there are the residual types (usually for two or three months) such as simazine and propachlor, which, if applied correctly, are strong enough to kill only germinating weeds so that they can safely be used among a wide variety of established plants such as roses and herbaceous subjects.

Weedkillers are normally sold in both solid form as granules or powders, and as a liquid to be diluted with water and applied with a sprayer or watering can with dribble bar attachment. For lawns they also come combined with a grass fertiliser and one springtime application is usually sufficient to ensure a clean, healthy lawn through the summer.

Most types are sold under trade names, but the packs must display the names of the active chemical ingredients. Also given are precise rates of application and safety instructions. Observe them at all times. Weedkillers are poisonous and some will kill humans as well as plants. Paraquat is a prime example. Keep all weedkillers well out of the reach of children and *never* store them in unlabelled containers.

Pelleted seeds eliminate the need for thinning out later

Construction

Some people hate it—others love it—but, whatever your feelings, it would be difficult to do without it. This sums up the role of concrete in the garden.

So what is this versatile material and how do you make and use it? Concrete is a mixture of cement lime, sand, gravel (coarse aggregate) and water; building mortar excludes the gravel. Ordinary Portland cement lime is grey, but it can be bought in different colours to improve the appearance of special work. It should always be dry before mixing and free from any lumps that cannot be broken easily with the fingers.

There are four basic mixes for garden work: A—for paths, pools, steps, edging and thin sections use one part by volume of cement, two of sand and three of gravel; B—for foundations, floors, drives, filling for rollers and thick walls use one part cement, $2\frac{1}{2}$ of sand and four of gravel; C—for formal or crazy paving less than 2in (5cm) thick and for mortar if you use builders' sand you will need one part cement and three of sharp sand; and D—a stiff mortar for bedding paving use one part cement and five of sharp sand.

Water is added to all of these mixes, small amounts at a time, until the concrete or mortar has the required consistency and all the ingredients are evenly mixed together. Small quantities should be mixed on a clean, hard surface or a platform of boards. If you need a large amount of concrete to lay a path or drive it is best to either order a load of ready-mixed or at least hire a concrete mixer from a do-it-yourself centre.

Before beginning to lay concrete it is essential to know how much of each ingredient to buy to make up the required amount. The volume is worked out by multiplying the area you want to cover by the thickness of the layer.

But whatever job you are going to do it is essential to get your levels correct before you start. These levels are marked by driving wooden pegs into either side of, and at regular intervals over, the ground you are going to cover; the tops of the pegs should be flush with the top surface of the concrete. Over short distances the pegs can be set by using a straightedge and spirit level. All you have to do is to get the top of the first peg at the required height and the spirit level will tell you when the subsequent pegs are flush.

When the distance involved is too great for this method, try this trick I picked up from a builder friend. Use a hosepipe, because water always finds its own level. Establish the first peg as before and tie one end of the pipe to it, open end uppermost exactly flush with the top of the peg. Take the other end of the hose to the furthest point of work and fix it loosely, end uppermost again, to another peg as near to the same level as the first one as you can judge it by eye. Pour water into the hose until it is full, raising or lowering the furthest end and topping up until the water comes to the top of the hose at both ends. Knock the furthest peg in until the top is flush with the top of the hose and it will be exactly the same level as the first one. The joy of this method is that it works over any distance—even round corners.

Making a path

Concrete It's not everyone's idea of a picturesque garden path, but if you want a serviceable, safe, clean surface to take you from one point to another, then concrete (mix A) is tailor-made. There is no need for it to look boring either, because while the concrete is still wet the surface can be lightly brushed with a stiff broom to give an interesting, non-slip texture, or brushed more strongly to expose some of the aggregate and give the appearance of rolled gravel.

After obtaining the level and excavating down to the level of the underside of the concrete, fill soft areas with hardcore and roll the whole length to compact it. Make a wooden framework the same depth as the required concrete along each side of the path and hold it in position by pegs on the outside. The concrete will be flush with the top of the woodwork so make sure that these levels are accurate. To shape the frame for a curve, make a series of saw-cuts half-way through the timber to allow it to bend.

Concreting can either be done continuously or by alternate bays. In either case the path should be laid in bays 8ft (2.4m) long with thin softwood cross lathes separating them in the case of continuous work or, if you are working in bays, simple butt joints to divide the surface into strips. This is because hardened concrete expands and contracts with temperature changes and might crack without these narrow gaps every so often.

Mix enough concrete for one bay at a time and spread it within the framework with a shovel, working it well

A simple butt joint is formed with the previous day's work. Note the hessian protecting the concrete (*Photo* Cement and Concrete Association)

into the sides and raking it down to within a quarter of an inch above the sides of the frame. Compact it with a punner or by working a board, slightly wider than the path, over the surface with first a chopping, then a sawing motion, resting the board on the frame sides. This ensures that the path surface is level, and finishing with a wooden float will give a smoother surface if required. Continue a bay at a time until the path is complete.

Paving Whether for paths or patios, all forms of paving can be bedded on concrete, sand, ash or compacted earth. Concrete is firmer and prevents grass and weeds from growing between the slabs. For a concrete base prepare the site by removing the topsoil and ensuring that the ground is firm and level. Keep edges straight with string lines. Bed the slabs, one at a time, in mortar (mix D) spread 1in (2.5cm) thick. Tap each slab into position, leaving a gap of $\frac{1}{2}$in (13mm) between them, until it is level, flush with the others and does not rock.

Fill the joints with mix C, ram well in and smooth with a trowel.

Alternative forms of bedding should be spread in a layer at least 2in (5cm) thick and compacted to keep it level. Earth should be well rolled. As each slab is bedded down, its level must be checked by means of a spirit level and straightedge, and adjustments made by adding or removing the bedding material. Fill the joints with sand or soil.

Crazy paving The use of irregular-shaped pieces of paving or stone laid at random is highly attractive in both old and modern-style gardens. The actual mechanics of laying are the same as for ordinary paving. Put down the outer edges first and work towards the centre, using pieces with straight edges for the sides of the path. Remember that if the pieces are placed together too carefully the result will look rather like a jig-saw puzzle and that sought-after random effect will be lost.

Laying a slab path

1   Roll the sub-base to ensure good compaction.

2   Check the levels for paving.

3   Spread the sand bed.

4   Roll and compact the sand bed.

5   Place five spots of mortar to receive the slab.

6   Tap the slab to line and level.

Building a wall

There are many different types of wall to be found in the garden, from a mere one or two foot retaining wall for terraces and raised beds, to tall dividers or screens of brick or open blocks. Except for the low ones they all require a solid, level foundation, of concrete at least 6in (15cm) thick and 6in (15cm) wider on both sides than the width of the wall.

To make the footings, mark out their line with pegs and string and dig out a trench to the required depth or until firm ground is reached. Drive in wooden pegs along the bottom of the trench, the tops set level to indicate where the surface of the footing should be. Fill the trench to the tops of the pegs with concrete (mix B), pack it down well and leave it to harden for at least a day, preferably more, before building starts.

It would be foolish for beginners to attempt anything higher than about 2½ft (75cm) until they are more proficient. A free-standing structure of this height in either bricks, stones or blocks should be at least 4in (10cm) thick and there should be a pier for stability every 10ft (3m) at least.

Whatever building material you choose, when laying spread a layer of mortar (mix C made fairly stiff) below and on one end of the block. Put it in position and tap firmly into place with the handle end of the trowel, checking the level as you go. Keep the joints to an even thickness. As the wall grows, check it vertically with either a plum bob or mason's level. To get the horizontal level correct, set one block at each end of the course and stretch a tight line across the top between the two, holding it in place with another block at each end. The remainder of the course can now be laid, lined up with the string, ensuring that joints don't occur directly above each other by starting each alternate row with a half block.

Bonded stone If you are using natural stone it will probably not all be the same size, so sort it to obtain courses of equal depth, or, alternatively, use stones of varying sizes to create a random effect deliberately, although finding levels will be more difficult.

Both natural and reconstituted stone can be pitched to give an attractive rock face. Mark a line ½in (13mm) from the face all the way round each block and chip away a section of the face along the line. Make sure that all cuts are level as these edges are used to align the wall.

Screen blocks Open screen blocks look attractive and introduce an element of mystery by allowing just a glimpse of what lies behind. To produce an even overall pattern they are normally laid one above another with continuous vertical joints. This means that some reinforcement is necessary, not only to hold the blocks together but also to bind them to the piers, which are essential. The reinforcement can either be in the mortar—a U-shaped piece of wire or a strip of expanded metal overlapping two blocks—or cast into the cavities of pilaster units. To get an idea of what the pattern will look like complete and of how many blocks will be required in each course, you can lay them out horizontally on the ground before starting to build.

Dry stone walls Building these is an acquired art, so start with a low retaining wall until you get the hang of it. Put down the footings and lay the first course, using the largest stones. Bed each one firmly down on about 2in (5cm) of finely sieved soil, packing more soil behind and between the stones. Each one should slope slightly backwards so that the entire wall is at an angle. Putting rockery plants between the stones helps to hold them together and gives a pleasing effect. It is easier to plant them as the wall is being built. The top of the wall can either be planted up in the same way or capped with large stones.

A mellow dry stone wall and stone steps—both enhanced by planting

1 Set the first post 2ft (60cm) in the ground and concrete it in. Use a spirit level to make sure it is upright both ways.

2 Using the capping strip of the panel, measure for the second hole and dig it out.

3 Fix the panel to the first post with 3in (7.5cm) nails. This first post should be nailed on both sides of the panel, which should be at least 2in (5cm) above ground level.

Erecting a panel fence

Screening is always a problem in the garden. If it's an instant screen you want, it will have to be fencing, and you can save money by erecting it yourself. Most fencing is sold in panel form, which is simplicity itself to put up.

4 Set the second post in the hole and nail it to the panel, which is supported on a couple of bricks until secured. The post should then be concreted in.

5 Erect the remainder of the panels in the same way, finally nailing on the capping strip and post caps.

6 The panels should be supported with lengths of timber until the concrete has set.

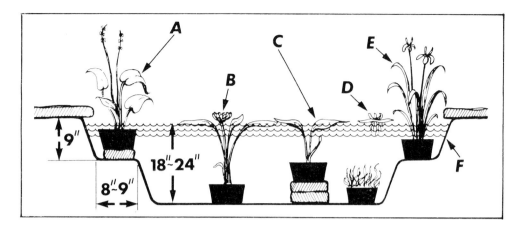

This cross-section of a typical pool shows how to plant aquatics correctly.

A A marginal requiring shallow water depth, with the container standing on a brick.

B Water lilies and deep marginals with fully extended foliage can be planted on the pool bottom.

C A newly planted deep marginal on a brick platform, which will be gradually lowered as the leaf stalks lengthen.

D Floating plants are useful for providing hiding places for young fish.

E Marginals requiring 5–6in (12–15cm) water depth can be placed directly on the marginal shelving.

F Pool sides slope inwards at 20° from the vertical; also note the 2in (5cm) overlap of paving at the rim of the pool which helps to prevent damage to flexible liners.

The basket beneath the floating plant D contains oxygenating plants like elodea (anacharis).

Making a water garden

A garden pool stocked with aquatic plants and fish can transform a static scene into a moving medley of colour, and the addition of a fountain or cascade heightens the effect. First decide what type of pool you need, whether a formal or a more natural-looking feature will blend better with its surroundings. A rock cascade and pool can enhance a rock garden, while formal pools are ideal for integrating into a patio design.

When siting the pool, always keep it well away from overhanging trees, particularly those like laburnum with poisonous fruits, or leaves and debris will soon foul the water. Ideally pools should be in full light, but healthy plant growth will be maintained if they receive sunlight for not less than half the day.

The most important point to watch is that all pool rims are absolutely level throughout their lifetime, to prevent seepage over the edge. This means that the base should be firm to avoid subsidence once the pool is filled—to be noted with concrete and large glass-fibre types.

The choice of materials comes next. For large pools incorporated into a system of rock pools and cascades, concrete is probably most practicable, but the foundations must be well prepared to prevent subsidence causing cracking. Rammed hardcore is required, and ideally 4–5in (10–12.5cm) of concrete (mix A) should be laid on this. Remember too, that the pool must be laid in one go. Waterproofing agents must be mixed with the concrete and the lime content must be neutralised by applying something like Silglaze before the pool can be stocked.

Moulded glass-fibre pools are useful for their strength, but although many styles are available, they cannot be obtained in very large sizes. This type of pool is durable and easy to install, and most firms offer cascades in the same material. Cheaper styles are also available in less durable, semi-rigid plastics.

Flexible liners are useful as they allow the imaginative gardener to create attractive shapes of any size. Several types of materials are available, their prices depending on their strength, and the longest-lived is butyl. Flexible liners come in rectangular sheets of standard size, but suppliers will join these up to make large pools to your specifications.

No pool should be less than 15in (38cm) deep or exceed 30in (75cm). For practical purposes most medium-to-large ones need a depth of around 18–24in (45–60cm). Ideally the sides should slope inwards at an angle of 20° from the vertical.

When laying flexible liners always make sure that the soil sides are free from sharp stones, or they may be punctured. Facing the sides with newspaper or discarded sheets of polythene will prove useful.

Plants and fish If you plant and stock your pool correctly, once established it will require little maintenance. Aim to get a balance between plants and fish so that the water will remain clear and contain sufficient oxygen for both.

Most aquatic specialists will provide collections of fish and plants for particular pool sizes, but if you want to grow a range of marginal plants it's best that the pool has a marginal shelf 8–9in (20–23cm) wide, otherwise the baskets holding the roots will have to be stood on bricks to keep them at the correct depth. Even the deep marginals are best started at a shallow depth and gradually lowered as the leaf stalks lengthen.

To get a balanced planting, choose one or two oxygenating plants that will grow in baskets resting on the bottom. Most people will want a water-lily or two, and there are many colours of both blooms and foliage. Other deep marginals can be planted if there is room, including the water-hawthorn (*Aponogeton distachyus*), which will grow in a water depth of 6–18in (15–45cm). Water violets can be similarly used and have the advantage of supplying oxygen to the water.

There is a wide range of side marginal plants to choose from, each plant preferring a particular depth of water. Those requiring shallow planting can be brought nearer the surface by placing the baskets on bricks on the outer shelving. The yellow double or single marsh marigolds (calthas) are happy in such positions, as are a range of water-irises, *Lobelia cardinalis* and bog- or buck-bean (*Menyanthes trifoliata*).

Be careful not to overstock your pool with fish. A guide to the amount the pool will hold is 2–3in (5–7.5cm) of fish per square foot (930sq cm) of surface available. Always allow the water to stand and the plants to become established before adding fish. A variety of carp, goldfish and bottom feeders like tench are always available.

Making a moulded glass-fibre pool with a cascade

1 After clearing the site, dig out the hole to the required depth, allowing an extra 6in (15cm) leeway round the pool.

2 Check the level of the rim in all directions and when this is correct, make sure the base of the hole is firm.

3 After firming, re-check the rim with a spirit level on a board. Then fill in round the sides with sand or soil.

4 Choose a cascade in a similar material and style to the pool and check that it is resting firmly on a soil or rock foundation before securing it with cement. Use a watering can to check that the flow is correct.

5 Ensure that the pump is correctly wired and that the plug carries the appropriate fuse. This submersible Otter pump runs directly off the domestic supply, but some makes need a transformer.

6 Note the special plastic baskets or crates supplied for planting aquatics. These are lined with sacking squares, filled with garden loam and topped with gravel.

7 After the pool has been planted, make the area surrounding it attractive. Here the rock garden was improved and bog and other moisture-loving plants added.

8 Check that the cascade inlet and the fountain work correctly before introducing livestock. If the hose is rigid, make it flexible by running warm water through it.

9 Allow the plants time to get established before introducing fish such as goldfish, golden orfe, tench and carp. Let the open bag float in the pool for several hours before releasing the fish.

Some of the wide range of accessories available for a garden pool and cascade, including baskets for plants and an Otter pump for aerating the water

Building a rock garden

Just because alpine or rock plants originate in the mountains it doesn't mean that a rock garden has to be a huge affair with massive great rocks and boulders. The art of rock gardening is to reduce a natural-looking mountain landscape to the scale you need—and this scale depends on the size of the area available.

The principle is the same for all sizes of garden: keep it looking as natural as possible. The site is important, so choose the best one before you start. Ideally it should be away from tall buildings and trees that cast heavy shade and give rise to drip problems in wet weather. Where shade-loving plants are wanted, they should be provided with nooks and crannies where rocks form small gullies and ravines, or they can be planted on the north side of larger stones.

To ensure perfect drainage, the ground should be dug thoroughly, taking care to remove any weeds, particularly the persistent types like bindweed, couch grass or ground elder. If the soil is heavy it will pay to put down a generous layer of hardcore in the second spit and cover this with a further layer of gravel. If you can lay this with a gradual fall to the front or one end of the bed, the water will tend to drain to one area, which will then provide a boggy patch ideal for moisture-loving rock plants like Primula rosea and some of the miniature musk varieties like Bees Dazzler.

Always try to follow nature's example by laying the rocks in strata with the grain of the stone running in the same direction. They do not have to run in horizontal terraces and some of the best features have a tilt to one side, copying the landslip pattern commonly seen in mountainous country. Where a large rock garden of any height is required, use the larger stones to form a solid foundation for the terraces above—these will act as an anchor and form a stable retaining barrier to the mass of soil behind. For planting a rock garden see page 66.

1 A length of hosepipe is ideal for marking out the shape of an island bed of medium proportions. Juggle small quantities of rocks to see which fit naturally together.

2   Remove the turf and dig over the site thoroughly to break up the soil and remove all weeds. If the soil is heavy, add hardcore in the lower spit to improve drainage.

3   Once the site is prepared, move the largest rocks into position. If a sack barrow is not available use rollers and a crowbar to avoid injuring yourself.

4   Group the largest rocks together and test for stability by standing on them. If they move at all they should be re-set. Anchor rocks on large features should be buried by up to two-thirds their depth.

5   Add or remove soil so that the rocks are completely stable. Ram the soil down well underneath to prevent shrinkage later.

6　Form outcrops or tiers of rock bays, giving the
tops of the stones a slight tilt back into the
bed for drainage. Try to achieve a natural strata
effect using grain of rock as a guide.

7　You should find that, after digging, quite a
large amount of soil will be spare for topping
up. Improve topsoil by adding peat, sharp sand
and grit.

8　Use the topsoil mixture to fill in terraces and
between rocks. Firm by gentle treading. Ram
soil into crevices between interlocking stones
to prevent air spaces.

Flowers

JANUARY
Jobs for the month
Mulch borders where spring-flowering plants are putting on new growth. Garden compost or proprietary types can be applied when the soil is not frosted.

In severe frosts, some less hardy plants like crinums may be damaged. Protect the crowns or bulbs by mounding up with dry peat, bracken or straw.

Early bulbs may be showing signs of growth. In exposed sites these may be scorched by cold and drying winds, so put down a protective covering of sand or weathered ashes.

Herbaceous perennials—the old reliables
Perennials are the permanent backbone of the flower garden, coming again just as good year after year—provided they are looked after. The hardy perennials that are left in the ground, cut down by the frosts and come again next year are truly the old reliables. By careful selection they can give up to a nine- or ten-month season of colour and interest.

Generally speaking, herbaceous borders and beds, or mixed displays containing them, prefer a sunny situation but there is still a wide choice for colder, shady sites. Except for the really spreading types it is best to group them in drifts of between three and five of the same sort, giving irregular, reasonably-sized masses.

Herbaceous borders need adequate drainage, so heavy ground will need plenty of ashes or grit worked in, while light, sandy soils will benefit from lots of moisture-retaining peat or humus of some sort. Well-rotted manure and compost is a good idea in all circumstances.

Here are just a few of the many herbaceous perennial plants, divided into three height groups, for the front, middle and back of the border.

Front (up to 2ft—60cm)   Dwarf asters (Michaelmas daisies), delightful bun-shaped clumps to 12in (30cm) high; dianthus (pinks and border carnations) is a versatile genus with many forms and colours, many of which have a lovely clove scent (the dwarf forms are excellent rockery plants); *Helleborus niger* (Christmas rose), white, winter flowering and *H. orientalis* (Lenten rose), pink and white, March and April; hostas are superb foliage plants for more

A front border of dwarf asters

moist parts of the garden with handsome variegated leaves; *Nepeta mussinii* (catmint) has attractive grey foliage and lavender or violet blooms from June to September; the species geraniums (cranesbills) are hardy perennials and give large clumps of flowers; potentilla (cinquefoil) has some nice low-growing hybrids with strawberry-like leaves and bright flowers in scarlet, orange, yellow and cherry; *Tradescantia virginiana* (spiderwort), from the same family as the popular Wandering Jew houseplant, is happy in any soil and situation.

Mid-border (2–4ft—60cm–1.2m) Achillea (yarrow) look better grown in groups; varieties of *Achillea ptarmica* give double white flowers; asters are also invaluable in this height range, particularly *Aster amellus, A. frikartii* and the *A. novi-belgii* types; campanula (bellflower) is a large and lovely genus and suitable types are *C. persicifolia, C. latifolia* and *C. latiloba*; of the hardy border types of chrysanthemums the best-known are the *C. maximum* varieties but many others give superb autumn flowers in a variety of colours and forms; *Delphinium elatum* (4ft, 1.2m) and *D. belladonna* (3ft, 90cm) give shorter versions of those beloved flower spikes in blues and pinks; *Gypsophila paniculata* gives exquisite misty sprays of tiny double flowers; lupin *(lupinus)* is probably best represented by the excellent Russell strains; *Lychnis chalcedonica* (Jerusalem cross) has round heads of scarlet flowers from June to August; peonies are among the most majestic of border plants in June and July; *Papaver orientale* (oriental poppy) offers brilliant colours in late spring; another bright subject is *Phlox paniculata* in many colours which 'holds the fort' in late summer until the autumn flowers arrive.

Back-border (4ft—1.2m—and over) Achillea filipendulina has flat heads of bright yellow flowers; *Aster novae-angliae* is the very tall Michaelmas daisy; delphiniums can give showy spikes up to 6ft (1.8m) in June and July; *Helianthus decapetalus* is the imposing sunflower with its huge golden heads towering several yards off the ground; *Kniphofia uvaria* (red-hot poker) is a favourite subject from July to September; other golden-yellow subjects are *Rudbeckia nitida* Herbstonne and the taller types of golden rod *(Solidago hybrida)*.

Making a start with dahlias
Starting old dahlia tubers into growth requires warmth and light. If an overnight temperature of around 50°F (10°C) is maintained, the old roots will start to develop new growth within a couple of weeks. A further two weeks and they will have become sizeable shoots, 2in (5cm) or 3in (7.5cm) long, at which stage they can be severed from the parent tuber and encouraged to grow roots of their own.

To start this cycle half-fill trays or pots with a mixture of peat and coarse sand. Place the containers over your heat source for a few days to warm up. After examining the over-wintered tubers for deterioration, push them firmly into the surface of the mix, allowing the crown (the point where the old stem meets the tuber) to stand clear of the surface of the compost. Refrain from further watering until growth is established.

Dwarf delphiniums in the mid-border

Opposite

For those with acid soils, azaleas are essential shrubs, providing great masses of almost every imaginable colour during spring. There are evergreen and deciduous varieties.
Overleaf Above A close up of part of a delphinum flower — those elegant spikes that grace the herbaceous border in summer. *Below* Freesias are among the most popular of florists' flowers, but they can be grown successfully by amateurs in heated greenhouses.

Clean up the herbaceous border

If the ground is not deeply frozen, clean up the herbaceous border, removing all dead stalks and any weeds that have grown over the winter. Improve soil fertility by adding fertiliser and organic mulches, and promptly suppress any pest outbreaks.

1   Cut off all dead stalks and foliage down to the crowns, but take care not to damage young shoots or overwintering buds. Firm down any newly planted subjects lifted out of the ground by frost. Thoroughly inspect spreading, mat-forming plants like snow-in-summer (cerastium) and remove any weeds that have come up and through the foliage.

2   Gently fork over the bed, taking care not to damage shallow roots or bulbs that are now making topgrowth. Remove weeds as you move along the bed.

3   An application of general balanced fertiliser will get herbaceous plants off to a good start when the weather turns warmer. Use a slow-acting granular type for preference.

4   On heavy ground, the addition of peat, garden compost and clay-breaking products like calcified seaweed will help to improve soil structure, giving better aeration and drainage.

5   Control any pests that may be active in mild weather. Watch out for aphids on violas and pansies and spray them if you see any pests. Put down slug pellets round other plants with new shoots emerging.

FEBRUARY
Jobs for the month
Tackle weeds before they can become established, especially under shrubs, where they can be seen more easily at this time of the year.

A good way to find out if your sweet pea seeds are viable before sowing is to pre-germinate them in the house on pads of moistened paper. After a week or so in heat they should germinate and once the roots show they must be potted up and placed in a cold frame or greenhouse.

If you were unable to plant lily bulbs outside last autumn they should go in now.

Fill any gaps in wallflower beds with spare plants and firm down any that have been lifted by frost.

There is still time to plant bergenias in a sheltered spot. One of the most popular species is *B. cordifolia,* which has rose-pink flowers, while *B. c. purpurea* is a deeper colour.

Herbaceous root cuttings
Thick-rooted herbaceous plants like gypsophila, oriental poppy, anchusa and phlox can be increased by taking root cuttings. They need a well-drained soil. Larger roots can be struck in the open ground, while small numbers are best in boxes or pots.

1 Lift some roots or, with plants like oriental poppies that resent disturbance, carefully scrape soil away and cut off mature roots with a knife or secateurs.

2 Cut roots into sections 1–3in long (2–8cm), at an oblique angle at the cut furthest from the crown if the roots are thick.

3 Insert, oblique cut first, into pots of sandy compost so that the tops are at soil level. Thin roots, like phlox, can be buried about $\frac{1}{2}$in (13mm) deep, laid horizontally. Give the pots a good soaking, then place them in a shady cold frame to root.

Early flowering alpines
Flowers on the rockery are always a welcome sight after the bleakness of winter and a number of plants will now be thrusting their flower buds upwards. During late February and March quite a lot of plants will give a cheerful display, providing, of course, that they are planted on the leeward side of the rockery away from the chilling north-east winds.

In a pocket of acid soil, *Polygala chamaebuxus purpurea* will often throw out the odd flower from mid-January. Another evergreen that also requires an acid soil is *Kalmilopsis leachiana* Le Pinic, which forms neat mounds some 6in (15cm) high and is covered with small lilac-pink flowers. For a pocket on the shady side of the rockery, in which the soil is only slightly acid, you can grow dwarf primulas which open in February and March; *P. rosea* Delight with stemless carmine flowers and *P. warshenewskyana* with brilliant pink flowers are outstanding.

For pockets in which the soil is on the limy side, why not try early-flowering saxifrages; *Saxifraga apiculata* forms domes of stiff leaves with light yellow flowers and *S. Jenkinsae* and *S. Irvingii* are hybrids that form domes of hard, grey-green leaves, the former having shell-pink flowers and the latter pale silvery-pink ones. Two early saxifrages that do not require much sunshine are *S. burseriana* Gloria, which has pure white flowers, and *S. oppositifolia* Latina, which has glistening pink blooms. Many of the early flowerers have short stems, which means that the flowers are often eaten by slugs. To help prevent this, grow them in pockets that are covered with 1in (2.5cm) of sharp grit.

Planted in a sheltered spot, aubretias will flower in late March. This genus is often decried as being too common but largely because many of the plants grown are seedlings and are often far inferior to many of the named cultivars that are available. Aubretia Dr Mules is a good old standby with masses of violet-blue flowers.

Saxifraga burseriana

1 Choose a sheltered, warm site in the sun where the soil is rich and well-drained. Plant tubers in groups towards the front of a border, or in rows for cutting, 4in (10cm) apart.

2 On heavy ground, add a little sharp sand to the planting holes. Tubers can be soaked overnight to make them swell or plant them direct from the packet, 2in (5cm) deep.

Planting anemones

St Brigid and de Caen anemone tubers can be planted in the open or in pots for a late spring and early summer display. Don't plant deeply and ensure good drainage. The de Caen type have large single flowers and the St Brigid have double or semi-double blooms.

3 Mark out the extent of the group to avoid damaging the shoots as they emerge in spring, then cover tubers and gently firm the soil with a rake head.

Anemone blanda Radar has wide open flowers, almost white at the centre and bright purple on the petals

MARCH

Jobs for the month

Delphinium seed can be sown from now until early summer in pans of compost. Sprinkle evenly but thinly, just cover, water, protect from light with paper until germination and place in greenhouse, cold frame or outside under a pane of glass.

The first planting of gladioli corms outside can take place at the end of the month, followed by further batches at three-weekly intervals to extend the flowering period. A covering of 6in (15cm) over the corm will be needed to prevent wind-rock later.

Snowdrops differ from other bulbous plants in that they can be lifted and divided as soon as flowering ends. This should be done every few years to prevent overcrowding.

Autumn-flowering hardy cyclamen such as *C. neapolitanum* can be planted now. They prefer cool, shady conditions and do well around the trunks of trees.

Some early herbaceous plants throw up more new shoots than they can support to eventual optimum flowering. Thin out to no more than six or seven of the strongest, using the others as cuttings if desired.

If soil conditions are right, plant out autumn sown sweet peas towards the end of the month, selecting short, stocky plants with at least one side shoot and clean white roots. Space 7–10in (18–26cm) apart.

Colour on the cheap

Bedding plants are fast gaining the reputation of being an expensive luxury. True, it costs a small fortune to buy enough plants to carpet a bed or border in early June as it should be done, and many amateur gardeners are finding the heating costs of raising their own bedders from seed in the greenhouse more and more prohibitive. But do you need a heated greenhouse—or even a greenhouse at all—to produce your own summer bedding plants by the hundred or even thousand? The answer is an emphatic *no*—there is nothing to stop you getting all the colour you want on the cheap.

Granted, you can't get the very best from some things—bedding begonias, lobelia, antirrhinums and a few others—without sowing them in a warm greenhouse in January or February. But there are a hundred other things that can be sown from the middle of March without any heat at all. They'll make grand plants to set out in your beds by the middle of June.

The cost will be the seeds, the compost and the boxes —that's all. If you've got a cold greenhouse, start sowing them mid-month. If you've got a cold frame wait until the end of the month. And if you've got neither, sow them on a windowsill in the house around the second week in April and stand them outside when you prick them out into boxes in early May.

Good bedding plants to sow this way from now on include alyssum, asters, dahlias, dianthus, helichrysum, impatiens, marigolds, nemesia, nicotiana, petunias, phlox, rudbeckia, stocks, tagetes, zinnias.

Sowing seeds of half-hardy annuals

1   No-soil compost is superior to anything else for raising seeds. It must be moistened before use by lightly spraying it with water and rubbing between the hands. The compost must be made uniformly firm and the surface flattened and made even with light pressure. Finish with the compost around $\frac{3}{4}$in (2cm) from the top.

2   Water thoroughly with a fine rose on the can, being careful not to disturb the surface, and allow to drain for a few minutes. The seeds must be distributed thinly and evenly. Very small seeds can be mixed with dry sand to make this job easier. If the seeds are large enough, place them individually $\frac{1}{4}$in (6mm) apart.

3   Large seeds need up to $\frac{1}{4}$in (6mm) of cover, but small seeds should be covered finely, so a fine sieve is essential. Cover with a piece of glass and sheet of newspaper, to prevent the surface from drying out, but move the paper as soon as the seeds show and prop the glass up by about $\frac{3}{4}$in (2cm). After a day like this, take the glass away completely.

Sowing hardy annuals direct

Another way to get a cheap and quick floral display is by sowing hardy annuals direct into the beds.

Mid-March or any time in April is plenty early enough. There are several ways of making these beds but all will be more effective if you first work out a rough plan on paper. It is better to aim at something informal with irregular patches or drifts of each subject. Study heights and colours from the information on the packets so that you can devise a colour scheme and position the tallest growers at the back—or in the centre of an island bed. The picture strip shows that quite ambitious patterns are possible but simple drifts are very effective. Thin out finally to 6in (15cm) apart.

With broadcasting you mark the bedding pattern, as shown in the picture strip, scatter the seeds, each variety into its own drift, and carefully rake them in. Either way it will be necessary to keep birds off the beds until the seeds germinate and the old method of criss-crossing black cotton tightly across the area between sticks is still the best. The resultant plants must be thinned out to at least 6in (15cm) apart.

Some of the varieties you should consider are:
Calendulas Commonly known as the pot or Scotch marigolds. A new dwarf compact strain is available called Fiesta Gitana. A mixture of colours and easy to grow.
Candytuft Dwarf varieties are around 9in (23cm) tall. Red Flash, a fairly new one, is about 12in (30cm) and there is a strong-growing white, hyacinth-flowered that can get up to 18in (45cm).
Clarkia Fairly tall and graceful growers from 18–24in (45–60cm).
Cornflower Dwarf varieties such as Polka Dot are 15–18in (38–45cm); others can be up to 3ft (90cm) and quite bushy.
Dimorphotheca Never more than 12in (30cm) high, but generally about 9in (23cm).
Echium Consistent at 12in (30cm).
Eschscholtzia Most varieties are around 12in (30cm) high, but Miniature Primrose is only 6in (15cm).
Godetia There are dwarf, medium and tall varieties from

Calendula officinalis **Fiesta Gitana**

6in (15cm) to 2ft (60cm). The more room they are given the more they bush out.
Larkspur Giant Imperials can tower up to 4ft (1.2m), but there are dwarfs down to 18in (45cm).
Limnanthes Real dwarfs at 6in (15cm), never more.
Linaria Neat little plants just under 12in (30cm).
Linum A very dainty, whispy 18in (45cm).
Love-lies-bleeding Careful with these—they can make 3ft (90cm) high and 2ft (60cm) across.
Mignonette Always around 12in (30cm) high.
Nemophila Makes a carpet 6in (15cm) thick.
Nigelia A dainty 15in (38cm).
Night-scented stock Always around 12in (30cm) high.
Phacelia P. campanularia is around only 9in (23cm) high, but there are one or two varieties more than double that.
Poppies Fairly consistent subjects at about 2ft (60cm) but there's a peony-flowered variety reaching 3ft (90cm) or more.
Sweet sultan A consistent 2ft (60cm).
Viscaria Blue Angel is a neat and compact 10in (26cm) but generally sold as a mixture up to 15in (38cm).

A border of eschscholtzia

Once the ground is dry enough to break down into a fine seed bed tilth, hardy annuals can be sown in the open. Choose a fairly open site to get strong, compact growth and sow thinly to avoid overcrowding seedlings, which would become straggly and poor flowering.

1   Break down large clods and rake the soil level, then apply a general balanced fertiliser at the rates recommended on the bag.

2   Rake in the fertiliser and remove any large stones as you get the soil into a fine tilth. Good drainage is needed.

3   Mixed annuals can be broadcast thinly over the area, but where several different types are to be grouped, dry sand can be used to mark the outline on the site.

4   Use these outlines as a guide to draw out 1in (2.5cm) deep drills, and sow the seeds evenly and thinly in these. Spacing between drills depends on the size of the annual sown.

5   Cover seeds with soil using a rake with teeth just breaking the surface. Draw the rake down towards you, then once more across the whole area.

6   Gently tamp the soil firm with the rake head. Mark out the extent of the groups with labels and finally water the area with a fine rose on the can if the soil is dry.

APRIL
Jobs for the month

Slugs and snails can be a real menace to newly emerging shoots, especially of plants like irises. Control them by putting down pellet bait treated with metaldehyde or methiocarb.

Spring-flowering plants like primroses and polyanthus are growing quickly; give them a quick-acting boost in the form of a liquid or powdered food.

Plants that suddenly droop for no apparent reason are probably being attacked from below soil level by insect pests like cutworms. Apply a soil pest killer such as Bromophos.

Many herbaceous border plants give better blooms if the shoots are thinned out now. Take out the smallest and weakest leaving the best well spaced out. Delphiniums, phlox and lupins particularly appreciate this treatment. Stir a little fertiliser in around the root area and mulch with manure, leafmould or peat.

Where staking is necessary in a border, it should be done as unobtrusively as possible. A cane to each spike is best for delphiniums, but if pea sticks are available push these in around plants and they will soon be hidden by the foliage.

Michaelmas daisies, heleniums, golden rod and many other herbaceous plants can still be divided and replanted.

The perennial scabious, so much valued for cutting, will divide and move well only in April. Dig up the root and split it carefully into pieces carrying one or two growing shoots. Water in after replanting.

This is not the time to divide irises. Take off dead leaves and very lightly fork in a balanced fertiliser. Moving time is after flowering.

Snowdrops can be divided now. Dig up where overcrowded and replant in small groups.

Pinks and border carnations like sunny, well-drained places. Fork in some wood ash if available.

New plants for rockeries are generally grown in pots and can be planted, even if in full flower. Take into account how far they will spread and be sure to include some that will flower in the latter part of the year.

Plants in ponds and pools can be divided now, so this makes it a good time to have a general clean-up. Drain or ladle water out and clear out all weeds and rubbish.

Rake balanced fertiliser into ground where chrysanths are going and be ready to plant any time from now on. Roots that have been out all winter will be growing now if still alive and will be best dug up and divided into single rooted pieces for replanting.

Established clumps of lilies can be top-dressed now with leafmould or peat. Lily seeds are best sown $\frac{1}{2}$in (13mm) deep and 1in (2.5cm) apart in pans or boxes and stood uncovered outside.

Bulbs for summer and autumn

Most gardens have at least a few spring-flowering bulbs, but how many have even a modest collection of summer and autumn-flowering bulbous plants? Very few, possibly because the best-known ones, such as gladioli and anemones, don't last long if left in the ground.

However, there are many bulbs covering a wide flowering period that can be planted from April onwards to bloom annually with only minimal attention.

Gladiolus Of the many different types available, the most practicable for the small garden are the butterfly group. Large-flowered varieties are ideal grown in bold groups in a large border and most colours are available. Gladioli must have plenty of sun and a rich, well-drained soil. Plant from April to May in batches for a succession of flowers. Plant the corms up to 4in (10cm) deep.

Anemone They require similar conditions to gladioli. The flamboyant de Caen and St Brigid varieties are colourful in the front of a sunny border and, if planted in succession from April until June, will flower from June to September.

The peculiar, claw-like tubers of ranunculus

Ranunculus This relative of the wild buttercup has 6–12in (15–30cm) stems topped by symmetrical double heads in a wide range of colours. Plant the odd, claw-like tubers claws downwards 2in (5cm) deep and 3–4in (7.5–10cm) apart in groups or rows and water copiously in dry weather.

Ranunculus flowers: brilliant double buttercups in a wide range of colours

Galtonia This is the summer hyacinth, with tall spires of white, bell-like flowers. The large bulbs are ideal for a mixed border, where once planted 5in (12cm) deep they need not be disturbed.

Lilium Less finicky about shade, but choosy about soil conditions, those lilies that flower late in summer are excellent in groups between shrubs or even in the herbaceous border. Most are lime-haters, however, and need a soil rich in humus. Species to try for a late show include *Lilium regale, L. auratum, L. henryi* and *L. speciosum*, all stem rooters, which means that bulbs should be planted at least 4–5in (10–12cm) deep.

Crinum powellii One of the last summer bulbs to flower and one of the most impressive. The massive bulbs, about 12in (30cm) long, including the tapering neck, and up to 5in (12cm) wide at the base, should be planted in a sunny, protected spot, leaving the top couple of inches protruding from the ground. Once planted, leave alone apart from a winter mulch of dried peat or bracken. Each bulb produces a stem 2–3ft (60–90cm) high topped by a cluster of up to ten pink or white trumpets, each 3in (7.5cm) across.

Lovely lilies: (above)late-flowering lilies are mainly lime-haters so grow them in pots if you're on chalky soil, or add plenty of peat to the planting site and rest the bulb on a mound of sand; (below) stem-rooting lilies like this *Lilium speciosum* require planting at least 4in (10cm) deep and in a partially shady spot

Colourful crinums: (above) once planted, these huge *Crinum powellii* bulbs can be left for years without disturbance; (below) the enormous pink or white blooms are produced in late summer

Tigridia Treat the Tiger Flower as for gladioli. Although individual blooms are short-lived, each plant will keep up a constant stream of iris-like blooms in the most amazing red, yellow or violet hues, beautifully marked by blotches in the centre of each chalice. Plant now 3–4in (7.5–10cm) deep in the sun and lift in autumn after flowering ceases.

Nerine bowdenii Blooming in the autumn, this nerine is the only species hardy enough to stand our winters. It should be planted 6in (15cm) deep, preferably against a south-facing wall. Leave undisturbed until the clumps get overcrowded. The 2ft (60cm) stems bear a cluster of delicate pink or red blooms.

Plant *Nerine bowdenii* in a sheltered, south-facing position, 6in (15cm) deep

Attending to bulbs

Don't allow your bulbs to suffer from lack of attention now they've finished flowering. Keep up the flowering power of snowdrops by dividing large clumps and allow other types to die down gradually.

1   Now that the snowdrops have finished blooming it's a good time to lift and divide any overcrowded clumps that have shown signs of soil exhaustion by flowering poorly.

2   You can replant individual bulbs to cover a large area, but a more immediate effect can be had next year by planting small groups of four or five offsets.

3   Potted bulbs of all types that have finished their display indoors can be put out into cold frames to die down, or plunged to their pot rims in a protected spot in the garden.

Three more lovely autumn-flowering bulbs should not be planted out until between July and September. These are the autumn crocus species, colchicums (naked ladies) and sternbergias. Plant the first two 2–3in (5–7.5cm) deep and sternbergias 6in (15cm) deep and leave them alone.

Taking lupin cuttings

Where you have a particularly fine form of lupin, propagating by seed will not give identical seedlings, so it will be necessary to take cuttings now. Remember to propagate only from the strongest and healthiest plants.

1 Small quantities of cuttings can be had by scraping soil from good plants in the border and carefully removing a clump of new shoots. Alternatively, completely lift plants.

2 Clumps of shoots are not easily separated from the main crown, so you will need a sharp knife. Individual shoots can be cut from the groups with a razor blade.

3 Make a slanting cut through the base of the shoots, making sure that some of the older crown growth is retained. Remove all dead or damaged foilage. Dipping the cut area in a combined fungicide/root compound will discourage rotting and help rapid root production.

4 Gently tap off excess compound and insert cuttings into pots or boxes filled with any well-drained compost. Water in and place in cold frame.

5 If you want to replant lifted lupins, trim back the thick tap root by half its length. Don't worry about wart-like nodules on the main roots. These are the homes of beneficial nitrogen-fixing bacteria.

MAY

Jobs for the month

Lupin cuttings that were taken in March should have produced strong roots and will need planting out in the herbaceous border. Beware of slugs, which damage the young growths at night.

Biennials such as Sweet Williams, Canterbury bells and antirrhinums should be sown for flowering next spring.

Container-grown pansies raised under cover from seeds sown last autumn can be planted in a cool but not too shady spot with rich, moist soil. They can be used as an edging to beds or grouped to give splashes of colour in borders. Allow 8in (20cm) between plants and don't bury the crowns too deeply.

Rock plants and alpines can be planted from containers into prepared soil pockets in the rockery. If it is full of persistent weeds like couch grass or oxalis, which are difficult to remove by hand, it is best to start again with clean soil. Many dwarf alpines are best sown when the soil is topdressed with sharp grit or small rock chips, which conserve moisture and suppress weeds.

Early-flowering chrysanthemums can be planted in prepared ground.

Later-developing herbaceous plants such as delphiniums need their shoots thinning out as before. Stake tall spikes as necessary in this border.

It is still a little too early to plant out rooted dahlia cuttings but the ground can be prepared now. Add rotted manure, compost or peat to the soil, as well as a general fertiliser dressing.

Dwarf lupin Lulu

Don't fall into the tender trap

May is the month when the new and inexperienced gardener can easily be tempted to spend unwisely on plants, particularly bedding plants. Although he may well buy the very best from a good source, because of over-anxiety in setting them out and possible ignorance of how they grow, he can easily lose the lot through planting out too soon.

Many of the bedders sold by the million at this time of year are half-hardy plants, which means that they can be killed off, or severely damaged, by frosts. With the possibility of frosts being around until the first week in June, there is a risk in planting them out before then.

On top of that, there is another risk. They have, of necessity, been raised in warm greenhouses, and are going to find conditions outside a bit hard for a start, whatever the weather. The earlier they are planted out, the less time they have had to be well hardened off in a cold frame, and the more likely they are to succumb to the change of environment.

The discerning buyer, if he sees good plants that he particularly wants, can buy them and set the boxes or pots in a cold frame or protected place for a week or two, until the safe planting time arrives. All he needs to do is to keep them watered.

Pansy F1 hybrid Sunny Boy

Planting a hanging basket

Hanging baskets are useful if there is little garden space. There are also half-baskets for fixing directly on walls or fences. Once planted, do not allow them to dry out, and feed them regularly once flowering commences.

1   If you choose a mesh basket, make sure the wire is plastic covered or galvanised to prevent corrosion. Put in a layer of moss to hide the polythene liner and soil.

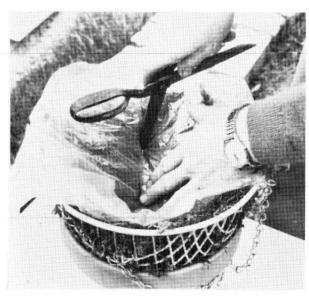

2   Nowadays polythene film is used to retain compost as it prevents soil from drying out better than moss alone. Make sure this is pierced to allow for drainage.

3   Knock out plants from their pots and check that there are no pests. Spray with insecticide before planting. Shown are ivy-leafed geraniums Pink Pearl. Other good trailers are lobelia, verbena, petunias, mesembryanthemums and pendulous types of begonias and fuchsias.

4   Partially fill the basket with a compost such as J.I. No. 2 or a peat type and position plants round the rim, slightly tilting the root balls inwards.

5   Fill in with more compost and gently firm between root balls allowing at least $\frac{1}{2}$in (13mm) space from rim down for watering. Trim polythene down to rim. Give basket, including the moss, a good soaking and keep in a warm, sheltered spot for a week or so to become established. Once frosts have passed, hang it up in a permanent position.

Planting dahlia tubers

Plant dahlia tubers in prepared sites from mid-May onwards. If you don't have much room, try the miniature Topmix varieties, which grow only about 12in (30cm) high. These are also good for tub planting on patios.

1 You can make two or more plants from a large cluster of tubers, provided each division has a bud or 'eye'. Use a sharp knife or razor blade. Wounds made in this way or by removing any rotted portions should be treated with sulphur powder or other fungicidal dust.

3 Plant tubers of miniatures 4in (10cm) deep and larger varieties about 5in (12cm) after forking the organic material into the base of the planting hole. Space plants 12–18in (30–45cm) apart.

2 Dahlias need a well-drained soil that doesn't dry out in summer. Rotted manure or compost dug into the site is beneficial, or add peat or potting compost to the hole.

4 Insert a stake to show the position of each plant to avoid hoeing off emerging shoots and treat the site with a soil pesticide before filling in with soil.

JUNE
Jobs for the month

You can propagate from violas or pansies by basal stem cuttings during this month and next, for planting out in autumn. Unless the material is sparse, avoid using old, straggly outer shoots.

Wallflowers sown in rows now will provide transplants ready for setting out in autumn, for a display next spring. They grow in most soils but avoid ground infected with club-root disease.

Any newly planted subjects must be kept watered until the roots have had a chance to establish themselves. This applies particularly to sweet peas and all varieties of bedding plants.

Trim back spreading rockery plants such as aubretia when they finish flowering to keep them tidy and encourage strong growth for next year.

As soon as delphinium and lupin flowers fade, cut off the seed pods. Your reward could well be a second display in August.

If you've never grown them before, winter-flowering pansies provide welcome colour in the dark months. Sow them now in boxes and stand in a cold frame. Prick out into more boxes and plant in their flowering position when well established.

Ivy-leaved geraniums are not only invaluable as trailers in hanging baskets, but they also make excellent carpet bedders. As they start to spread, peg the stems down with U-shaped wires.

Ageratum Bouquet (*Photo* W J Unwin Ltd)

Cordon-trained sweet peas will need attention as they reach their best. Tying up and de-shooting will be required twice weekly, plus a fortnightly spraying with derris to prevent a greenfly build-up. Water well in dry weather and apply a mulch over moist ground.

Sow seeds thinly of the old-fashioned Brompton stock. Transfer seedlings to flowering position in November or, on heavy soils, overwinter in a frame and set out in March.

Get bedding heights right

At last it's safe to plant out those bedding annuals. The secret of getting the beds and borders to look right is to have a good idea of what the overall effect is going to be at flowering time. Most bedding plants are approximately the same size in the boxes, with hardly any indication of how tall they will grow or how much of a spread they will make. Lobelias, for instance, will be about the same as asters, say, in the boxes, but get a carpet of 4in (10cm) high lobelias with a row of 18in (45cm) high asters round the outside and the effect would be ridiculous.

If you've sown and grown your own from seed, you can always get the information you need from the packet. But if you're buying boxes of plants to mix together, be sure you know what's what. Most people worry about colours, but this is nothing like as important as getting the heights right. This is further complicated by the fact that there are dwarf, medium and tall varieties of most things.

Marigolds can be 4in (10cm) or 24in (60cm), and asters are the same. Nicotianas can be less than 1ft (30cm) or as much as 3ft (90cm) high. There's a fairly new helichrysum that's only 1ft (30cm), when before that they had always been 3ft (90cm) or so.

Top of the bedding pops

Ageratum   This used to be a fairly uneven growing edger at around 9in (23cm). Now the F1 hybrids have given us real compact and consistent dwarfs at 5in (12cm). Make sure you know which you have.

Alyssum   Not much to worry about with these—3–4in (7.5–10cm) high is the limit with the white ones. Some of the pinks and purples are a little looser growing, and, of course, there's the yellow perennial variety Saxatile. Don't try to edge with that.

Anchusa   There's a beautiful dwarf annual variety of this called Blue Angel that's perfect for bedding at 9in (23cm) high. Don't get it mixed up with the perennial Italica that reaches up to 5ft (1.5m).

Antirrhinum   Never take these for granted. Types are never ending. They range from 4in (10cm) dwarfs to 4ft (1.2m) giants, with everything in between. Must be watched carefully.

Arctotis   There's a type of these called Grandis that needs 2ft (60cm) between them, and they're 2ft high.

Asters   A new range of dwarf bedders has appeared in the past few years, perhaps the best of which is Pinocchio at 4in (10cm) and, of course there are the giants, mainly used for cutting, at 2ft (60cm) high. Dwarfs are neat, tidy growers; giants are a bit unruly.

Begonia semperflorens

Begonias   Like the antirrhinums, there are infinite varieties. The fibrous rooted kinds used for bedding range from the compacts at 6in (15cm) up to the normal 9–12in (23–30cm). Don't forget that among the tuberous varieties, also sometimes used for bedding, are pendulous kinds, suitable only for baskets, tubs, etc, where they can trail over the sides.

Plants that have been in boxes or pots too long never recover properly and never reach their true dimensions. These antirrhinums are not worth planting out

Calceolarias The hardy ones that we plant outside are *C. rugosa*. Don't get them mixed up with the indoor pot varieties.

Centaurea macrocephala

Centaureas These are the silver leaved plants that get to 18in (45cm) high and the same across in a good season.

Chrysanthemums A lot of confusion about these when they are offered as bedding plants. Those grown from seed are annuals. They have finely-cut, fern-like leaves and daisy flowers in several colours. Height up to 30in (75cm). There is also a strain called Early Flowering Charms that can grow up to 3ft (90cm) across.

Cineraria maritima Another silver leaved plant. Silverdust is particularly dwarf at around 6–8in (15–20cm).

Clary This needs careful placing. A bit taller than the average bedder at around 18in (45cm).

Convolvulus We all know the climbing weed only too well. But there are two beautiful annual relations used in beds. Major is a climber that will reach 8ft (2.4m). Minor is a compact bedder of 12in (30cm). Don't get them mixed.

Cosmea These beauties always grew to around 4ft (1.2m), but there are several new varieties now only half that height. Bright Lights is one, and very good too.

Dahlias Nothing is more variable than these. Never plant any without knowing how high they will grow. The dwarf bedding varieties start at about 18in (45cm); Redskin and Rigoletto are 15–18in (38–45cm); Coltness hybrids are 2ft (60cm) and from there on they can be anything up to 6–8ft (1.8–2.4m).

Dianthus Bedding varieties are fairly consistent from 6–9in (15–23cm) high and about the same or more across.

Gazanias These sunshine-lovers reach about 9in (23cm) high, but will branch out to make a bush 15in (38cm) across.

Geraniums Most of the new seedling varieties have been chosen for their good habits; they are 12–18in (30–45cm) high as a rule and bush out nicely in proportion. Older plants kept from one year to another can, of course, be grown to any size.

Helichrysum Hot Bikini is a super new dwarf variety. Bushes out nicely to 12in (30cm) across and is about the same high. Older varieties are used more for cutting and reach 3ft (90cm).

Heliotrope Very variable from seed so far as habit is concerned. Around 15in (38cm) high but can be anything across. The consistent plants grown in park beds are raised from cuttings.

Hollyhock There are some surprising new annual varieties that can be bedded and reach only 2ft (60cm)— Silver Puffs is one. Don't get them mixed with some of those 8ft (2.4m) giants.

Impatiens F1 hybrid Busy Lizzies are consistent in height and habit and will make neat beds almost anywhere. Older varieties are more variable.

Kochia Burning Bushes are much influenced by the richness or otherwise of the soil. They can stay at around 2ft (60cm) or will get to 5ft (1.5m).

Cosmea Goldcrest (*Photo* W J Unwin Ltd)

Lavatera Beautiful, but only for places with lots of room, 2–4ft (60cm–1.2m) high and need at least 2ft (60cm) between plants.

Lobelia No trouble, always neat, always compact, except those known as basket or pendula types.

These marigolds are just at the right stage and will go on developing to their proper height and spread without check

Marigolds Great care needed when planting these, because there are so many of them. They are consistent within themselves, but take care when mixing varieties. The dwarf French start at 6in (15cm) with the Petite strain and move up to 8–10in (20–25cm) with the dwarf doubles. African varieties can be anything from 10in to 3ft (25–90cm), and Afro-French about 12in (30cm).

Newly planted summer bedding plants invariably need watering in

Mesembryanthemum Flattest grower of all, but spreads rather variably.

Nasturtiums Another to be careful with. Trailers and climbers will travel 6ft (1.8m) or more. Dwarfs make small 6–9in (15–23cm) round bushes and semis get to around 15in (38cm).

Nemesia No worries about these. Dwarf strains are about 8in (20cm) but the tallest are only around 12in (30cm). They bush out better if plants are young when set out.

Nicotiana The new varieties are lovely bedders. Crimson Rock is even at 18in (45cm) and Dwarf Idol is less than 12in (30cm)—rather different from the 3–4ft (90cm–1.2m) Affinis that is still around.

Pansies Always 6–9in (15–23cm) but some strains are neater growers than others.

Petunias Not much in height, always 6–10in (15–25cm), but variable in habit. Some are more compact than others. Some strains are particularly rain-resistant. Looser growing varieties are the ones to get for tubs and baskets.

Phlox drummondi The annual phlox is a good spreader from 6–10in (15–25cm) high.

Rudbeckia The coming of the Rustic dwarf and Marmalade varieties revolutionised this flower. At 15–18in (38–45cm) they are different from the old Gloriosa daisies that flopped around at about 3ft (90cm).

Salvias Many new varieties are appearing, but not much in them to upset bedding schemes. Dwarfs are around 10in (25cm), others up to 15in (38cm). Watch for a type called Farinacea, which has 2½ft (75cm) spikes of blue flowers. Quite different from the ordinary types.

Stocks Giant stocks can be up to 2ft (60cm). Bedding strains are around 12in (30cm).

Tagetes Consistent edgers. The dwarf Paprika is only 5in (12cm), but most others are around 9in (23cm).

Dividing bearded irises

Allow at least a month's breathing space after flowering before dividing overcrowded bearded irises (flags)—this gives the rhizomes a chance to develop some new roots. Dwarf types can be lifted early in the month, followed by the intermediates later this month and the tall-stemmed ones in July.

1   Poor flowering is a sure sign that irises are overcrowded. Where rhizomes are 'climbing' over each other, lift and divide to keep the clumps in good condition.

2   Cut off large old rhizomes that don't carry leaf fans, but retain young ones that carry new roots and foliage. Remove any dead or damaged roots and foliage.

3   Reduce leaf fans using scissors. This will help to prevent rhizomes being lifted out of the soil before the roots are established and reduces water loss in the early stages of growth.

4   They prefer a neutral to slightly alkaline soil and drained, sunny conditions. Apply rotted manure or compost, plus a long-acting fertiliser like hoof and horn. Plant so that the leaf fans all face in the same direction with the rhizomes facing south for preference.

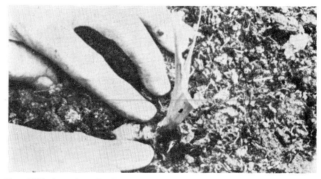

5   Fill in the hole so that tops of the rhizomes are above soil and firm gently on clay soils, more thoroughly on light, sandy or humus types of ground. Water in if the soil is dry.

Caring for the summer pool

This is the time of year when a garden pool really comes alive. Keeping both plant and fish population healthy should require little effort, except to maintain the all-important natural balance of the pool.

In the main this will consist of removing any excess plant growth to prevent overcrowding, as well as maintaining a constant water level by topping up during the hottest periods. But there are other jobs that may need attention from time to time.

In new pools especially, a build-up of free-floating algae may make the water cloudy. This will normally clear itself in balanced pools where planting has been done with care, and rarely worries pools over 40sq ft (3.4sq m) in area. It can be a recurring problem, however, in small pools, where it obscures fish and looks unsightly. This is a harmless condition often called 'green water'—even though it is sometimes reddish—and fish revel in it.

The common practice of siphoning off some of the water and adding fresh is not advised, as this usually results in the reappearance of the trouble soon after. It's far better to try one of the chemical algicides like Acurel 'E' or Algimycin PLL, which are harmless to fish and plants. An alternative is to install a pool filter.

Another type of algae that is particularly troublesome early in the season is blanketweed. This can choke a small pool in no time at all and is best removed by poking a stick into the mat of filamentous growth and twirling it round like candyfloss. Again the addition of algicide to the pool may help to control its growth.

Some ornamental plants may also get out of control and require thinning out. Nets are useful for scooping out the rampant surface floating plants like lemna (duckweed) but tougher plants in baskets may need to be cut through with an old knife blade or a razor blade on a cane.

Dead or fading foliage is also best removed before it decays and sinks to the bottom, except perhaps where a large expanse of water prohibits this.

Keep it topped up Topping up periodically will be necessary to replace up to 2in (5cm) of water lost each week through evaporation in summer. This is particularly important to plastic-lined pools, which can become brittle if exposed to long periods of bright sunlight.

The hose also comes in handy for aerating the water if no cascade or fountain is installed. A forceful jet played on to the foliage of water lilies infected with blackfly or lily beetle will wash these nasties into the water where the fish will make short work of them. On no account try to spray the plants near or in pools with insecticide.

Looking after your fish In hot weather the fish may come to the surface and gulp air. This is a sign of oxygen deficiency in the water and spraying over the surface with the hose, especially in late evening, will give some relief. But the installation of a cascade or fountain will give a more permanent method of increasing the oxygen content of the water.

Overstocked pools may also give similar trouble, with the smaller fish showing distress first. Overcrowding can also result in a disease, so it pays to keep to the recommended rate of 2–3in of fish length for every square foot of surface area.

JULY

Jobs for the month

Iceland poppies will provide a good colour show for border display or cutting if sown in any spare piece of ground this month. These biennial plants are discarded after flowering, but can be maintained by sowing annually. Young plants can be put into beds or borders in autumn or the following spring. They will give a long show of white, pink or red blooms in late spring and summer.

Perennial seedlings sown last month should be pricked out into boxes or transplanted to where they are to flower.

You can sow your own saved pansy seed, or start with a good strain sown either directly into a bed or in containers. Plants sown now will still be ready for planting in autumn. Later sowings are best put out next spring. Apart from F1 hybrids, seed from good strains can be harvested as the capsule splits and either stored in a cool place or sown immediately into crocked pans or boxes of rich compost.

Pipings of pinks

Once pinks have finished flowering they can be increased by using the basal shoots as cuttings (commonly called pipings). These will be planted out into their flowering quarters in September or overwintered in pots under a cold frame.

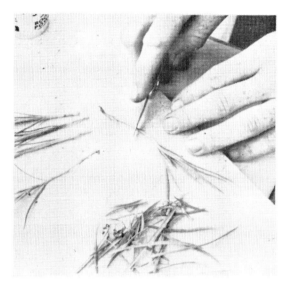

2 Remove some of the lower leaves, taking care that the small buds at the joints are not damaged, and trim back long stems, cutting just below a leaf joint.

1 Detach the pipings from the parent plant by giving a sharp pull. Take only from healthy, strong-growing plants.

3 Treat the end with a hormone rooting compound and space five or six pipings round a small pot filled with a sandy compost. Water in and root in a closed propagating frame. Keep shaded until roots form and then ventilate.

Poppies: (above) a group of Stormtard poppies; (left) a fine example of an Oriental poppy, Curtis strain

Disbudding flowers—and trapping earwigs

Some gardeners prefer their chrysanths and dahlias as large sprays of smallish flowers, but others like just one large flower. To achieve this the plants must be disbudded. The earwig problem can be dealt with at the same time.

Dahlias and chrysanths generally make a lot of flower buds, which is all very well if you want small flowers in sprays. If you want bigger flowers on long, straight stems, however, the little side buds can be taken off, leaving just the one at the top. This is the terminal bud.

Earwigs will eat the flower petals of both plants but as they crawl into dark places in the daytime they can easily be trapped. Put some dry grass in a 3in (7.5cm) pot. Rest the pots upside-down on canes along the plants. Earwigs will go into them and can be tipped out and killed every day.

AUGUST
Jobs for the month

The winter-flowering pansies sown in June will be ready for pricking out and planting where they are to flower in October.

Sow hardy primulas and meconopsis in well-drained soil in a sheltered, shady border. In cooler parts of the country they can be sown into boxes in a cold frame.

Among the most popular everlasting flowers are helichrysums; this variety is Hot Bikini, a Fleuroselect Bronze Medal winner in 1977. To dry the flowers, cut them and hang them upside-down for a fortnight

Late in the month is the time to cut 'everlasting' flowers such as helichrysum for drying. Tie them by the stems into bunches and hang upside-down in a cool, dry place. Keep out of direct sun or the flower colours will fade.

When lavenders have finished flowering, clip the bushes back or they will become leggy and appear bare at the base.

Arum lillies that have been dried off can be re-started. Repot the rhizomes, one to a 6in (15cm) pot or three triangularly in 8in (20cm) or 10in (25cm) pots. Stand outside until September, when they go into the greenhouse.

Take cuttings of *Iberis sempervirens*, ordinary and lemon-scented thyme, and ordinary or purple-leaved sage. They should be side shoots of the current season's growth with a heel of older wood. Insert direct into sandy soil in a cold frame or into pots or boxes.

Looking after potted bulbs

Don't make the mistake of neglecting bulbous flowers after flowering has finished. This is the time when many are forming buds for next year's display, so ensure that they are well fed or ripened off.

Growing summer bulbs will benefit from weekly feeds of balanced fertiliser. Bulbs such as these that have finished flowering but with foliage still in growth also need feeding, and the occasional overhead spray.

Where the foliage is dying down, gradually withold watering to encourage the plants to rest. Once foliage has completely dried up, bulbs requiring ripening, like these veltheimias, can be exposed to full sun and the pots turned on their sides.

New primulas from offsets

Where *Primula auricula* and *P. pubescens* varieties are becoming overcrowded with offsets it's not too late to reap a batch of new plants. The offsets in many cases will already have a small root system; alternatively treat as stem cuttings.

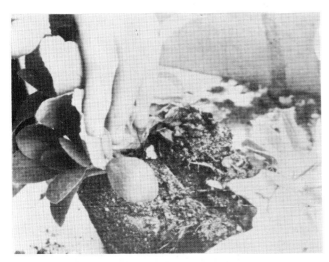

1 After carefully lifting plants or knocking them out of containers, give a gentle tug to part offsets from the parent plant or use a sharp blade to sever them from the main stem.

2 Trim off the old stem base, taking care not to cut off any roots. Unrooted offsets will take, but will establish at a slower pace.

3 Dust the wounded part of the stem with rooting powder containing fungicide or sulphur powder to prevent rotting.

4 Trim off dead or faded foliage and the base of the parent plant. Repot the parent using a little fresh compost containing sand.

5 The offsets will need a small pot, crocked for drainage. Use the same compost and plant so that the crown of the cutting is at compost level. Place in a cool, shady frame to get established before winter.

SEPTEMBER
Jobs for the month
Those lilies that produce miniature bulbs (bulbils) up the stem can be propagated now. Treat the bulbils like seeds and prick off into deeper containers when leaves appear next spring. Bulbs will build up to flowering size in about two years from 'sowing'.

Some annuals can be sown now for early blooms in May and June of next year. They include calendula, godetia, larkspur, nigella, Shirley poppies, annual scabious and coreopsis. Sown in the open, they should be well established before the cold weather arrives.

Sweet peas can also be sown now and over-wintered in a frame. Mice may have to be kept from them by frames with small-mesh wire netting.

Dahlias are now giving a colourful show, but if you want the display to continue until the frosts they must have regular feeding, watering and pest control. Large varieties, especially those with heavy blooms, will need supporting with canes.

Spring bulbs
The best time to plant   Bulb planting time for a spring display is from the beginning of September to around the end of the year. The early weeks of the period are the best, if only because planting conditions are likely to be better. There is an almost unlimited range of subjects to give colour from January until the end of May.

Bulbs in containers   Bulbs are ideal for containers, fitting into the wide choice of tubs, troughs and planters now available. Even where there is no garden you will find them in windowboxes and on patios and balconies. Being virtually self-contained units, all they need is a few inches of compost.

An idea to prolong the flowering time in, say, a windowbox is to first plant with early flowerers, and to have later subjects growing in pots or boxes elsewhere, ready to move in when the first are finished. They transplant well. Early crocuses followed by dwarf tulips would make an ideal combination. Drainage holes are necessary in all outdoor containers, with stones or crocks placed over them to prevent clogging by the growing compost. It is even possible to set bulbs in two layers, as long as they are not directly on top of each other. They will all flower at the same time if of the same variety.

Natural planting   Many bulbs are suitable for informal planting in such areas as grassy banks, beneath trees or shrubs, on the lawn or in wild places in any garden. Straight lines and rows are out—the bulbs must be scattered and planted just where they fall. Crocuses are real eye-catchers in drifts among grass. The blue of the grape hyacinth looks marvellous underneath *Magnolia soulangeana*, which flowers at the same time. Snowdrops associate perfectly with evergreen shrubs, and golden narcissus and scillas are never better than under the graceful silver birch.

Bulbs in the rock garden   The miniature bulbs are 'naturals' for the rockery, where their beautiful small

White snowdrops in the rock garden

flowers can be examined and appreciated at close quarters. First to flower, in January if the weather is kind, are the snowdrops and yellow winter aconites. Give both a shady sheltered pocket. A sunny spot is needed for the lovely dwarf irises, *Iris reticulata* and *I. danfordiae*, whose blue and yellow flowers appear in February. This is the time too when the Spring Snowflake (*Leucojum vernum*) is in bloom, and the first of the miniature narcissi, 3in (7.5cm) high *Narcissus minimus*, 6in (15cm) *N. cyclamineus*, and the 10in (25cm) golden Tenby daffodil (*N. obvallaria*).

By March there is a wealth of colour and variety—the sky blue *Anemone appenina*; the blue, pink, mauve and white flowers of *A. blanda*; the blues of the Glory of the Snow (chionodoxa) and of the puschkinias and scillas. The dwarf tulips also begin to open up, the Kaufmanniana varieties, the multi-flowering heads of *Tulip praestans* and the scarlet *T. eichleri* are all 9–10in (22–25cm) high, just right for a pocket of colour. So too are narcissi, the yellow Hoop Petticoat (*Narcissus bulbocodium*) being the best-known.

In April, grape hyacinths, dog's tooth violets and the fritillaries are in bloom, as well as another popular dwarf narcissi, *N. triandrus-albus* (Angels Tears), and May sees the main group of tulips plus alliums, ornithogalums and sparaxis.

Planting small bulbs

1   Before planting, check all bulbs for firmness. Discard any that are soft and showing signs of rot. Those illustrated are miniature narcissus.

2   Small bulbs are effective set out in groups on the peat bed, rock garden or in troughs. Where the soil is soft, use you fingers to make 3in (7.5cm) deep holes.

3   Allow at least 1½in (4cm) between the smaller bulbs, but up to 4in (10cm) for vigorous types like muscari. Plant 'nose' or neck upwards.

4   Small bulbs or corms like crocus look attractive when naturalised in grass. Scatter handfuls where you want a splash of colour and plant where they fall—but keep off main access areas where they will be trampled on.

5   Use a trowel to lift out a plug of turf 3–4in (7.5–10cm) deep. Alternatively, lift small squares of grass and space out bulbs in groups of holes in that area.

6   Add a little sandy compost to the hole and rest the base of the bulb on this.

7   Replace the turf plug or square and firm down, using your foot or a wooden tamper. Label the area to prevent emerging shoots being damaged next spring.

OCTOBER

Jobs for the month

Michaelmas daisies are useful for a late show when most other border plants have finished. Where you've pulled out old clumps—often those terrible, weedy, self-sown seedlings—rejuvenate the soil and plant some of the attractive modern named varieties. Whatever you do, always cut off faded flower heads to prevent a takeover by seedlings in the future.

Now that the summer bedding is finished, it's time to clear out the spent plants and replace them with something bright and cheerful for spring. Wallflowers sown earlier can fit the bill perfectly, especially if inter-planted with tulips of a contrasting or complementary colour. Before planting wallflowers, apply a general fertiliser to the ground at 3–4oz per sq yd (90–120gm per sq m). Dust the planting holes with calomel to help prevent club-root disease.

In all but the mildest parts of the country gladioli need lifting and storing in a frost-free place. Carefully lift the corms with a fork, cut off the stems to leave a neck 1–2in (2.5–5cm) long and allow to dry off on a sunny windowsill for a day or two. Many corms will have produced tiny offsets (spawn) that can be kept for 'sowing' next spring. Dust corms with a fungicide powder and store in a dry, cool place.

Divide lily clumps

Established liliums, particularly the modern hybrids, will become overcrowded about three years from planting, so to avoid poor flowering, lift and divide the bulb clumps as the tops die back. Fresh bulbs can also be planted in well-drained soil. Make sure you get the types that suit your soil, as many stem-rooting liliums are intolerant of lime.

1   Carefully lift overcrowded lilium clumps with a fork and remove dead or damaged scales. Look out for black slugs, which can work their way into the bulbs.

2   Take out a planting hole after forking the site over and removing weeds. Make sure the lower part of soil is thoroughly drained by loosening it with a fork and, if necessary, adding gravel.

3   Add a generous layer of humus material to the hole—peat, compost or something similar.

4   Plant the bulbs in a 'nest' of sand if the ground is heavy. Plant stem-rooting kinds at a depth of 8–10in (20–25cm) and basal rooting types 4–6in (10–15cm) deep.

5   Cover the bulbs with more humus or a little compost before filling up with topsoil. Gently tread the ground firm and mark the site with a label to avoid damaging emerging stems.

Make a plant container

If you're looking for a way of brightening up a windowsill, back yard or patio in spring, containers planted up with bulbs and spring bedders are excellent. The choice here is Golden Harvest daffodils with polyanthus.

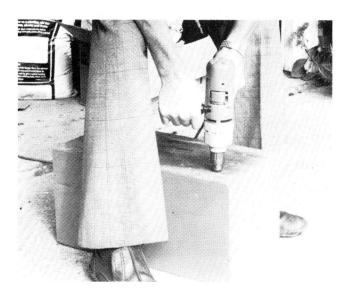

1   Plants in containers need good drainage, so drill out holes if none are provided. Use a masonry bit on pottery or reconstituted stone.

2   Give wooden containers a longer lease of life by treating the inside with a green wood preservative and paint the sides with wood varnish or a suitable gloss.

3   Add a generous layer of broken pot or gravel to prevent compost blocking the drainage holes. Cover this with some coarse peat. Partially fill with a well-drained compost and firm down, making sure not to miss the corners.

4   Space out the plants (polyanthus in this case) evenly in the box, and inter-plant with suitable companion plants like narcissi, hyacinths or tulips.

5   Top up with compost so bulbs are covered by twice their own depth and crowns of bedding or herbaceous companions are at soil level. Allow an inch or two at the rim for watering.

NOVEMBER

Jobs for the month

Young container-grown plants of kniphofias (red-hot poker) can be planted in groups, spacing them out no less than 18in (45cm) apart in the case of the shorter types and up to 6ft (1.8m) for the giants. Set out in well-prepared ground they need little care, but newly planted groups should be kept moist and given a protective coat of bracken or straw litter.

Protect established plants from frost by drawing up the dry foliage over the crown and tying it up to form a thatch.

The glistening white trumpets of the Madonna lily (*Lilium candidum*) are an important part of the cottage garden scene. The evergreen bulbs can be planted now, provided the ground isn't waterlogged or frozen, with the tip of the bulb lying just below the surface with the foliage above. This plant is a lime-lover, so it's ideal for chalky soils unsuitable for many other lilies.

Tulip bulbs can be planted and there is still time, early in the month, to put in daffodils and hyacinths if you forgot last month.

Stems of outdoor chrysanths should be cut back to a few inches and the roots lifted and boxed into compost, to be kept in a cold frame until around mid-December.

Replant lily-of-the-valley

There are few hardy plants that conjure up the 'good old days' more than the fragrant, nodding sprays of lily-of-the-valley. To ensure good flowering, give established clumps a generous organic mulch and see they are not overcrowded.

2 Replant in a new site, or enrich the existing one with compost, rotted manure or leaf soil. Give the ground a sprinkling of bone meal and fork over the topsoil.

3 Trim away dead or damaged roots before planting. Plants like a cool, shaded position that does not dry out in summer.

1 Overcrowded clumps will not flower well, so lift carefully and divide up the roots into single healthy crowns, each of which should have a strong bud at the base.

4 Plant the crowns about 3in (7.5cm) apart and deep enough to bring the tip of the bud just under the soil surface. Ensure that they do not dry out while making new roots.

Dividing herbaceous plants

Divide herbaceous plants that have outgrown their positions or have flowered poorly. Where the bed needs a complete overhaul, it's best to lift all the plants, then dig over the whole area thoroughly, adding compost and rotted manure before replanting divisions.

1 First harvest seed heads where they are needed for dried flower arrangements or seeds for increasing stock. If they are wet, dry them rapidly in a warm place to prevent mould.

2 Lift clumps that have become infested with perennial weeds and break them up to clean them thoroughly. Old overcrowded plants that have flowered poorly should also be divided.

3 Use two forks placed back-to-back to divide thickly matted clumps. Replant only young, vigorous divisions from the outside of the clumps.

4 If you intend to start planting a herbaceous border next spring, dig over the site and leave it rough. Add one of the proprietary 'soil breakers' on heavy clay soils.

Planting a rock garden

When you come to plant up your rock garden try to balance the low-growing plants with dwarf shrubs and make a selection that will give a succession of interest throughout the year. Summer flowering alpines with a mat habit are ideal for under-planting with a variety of the smaller bulbous subjects like crocus, narcissus and scilla species.

Evergreen shrubs like the slow-growing dwarf junipers and Japanese holly (*Ilex crenata*) are particularly useful for a continuous display, but take care not to plant quick-growing or rampant subjects in restricted areas.

Before actually planting, set out all the plants in groups in the most ideal situations for healthy growth. Use dwarf shrubs to give height on flat areas and station mat-forming alpines at the tops of outcrops where they can cascade naturally down the faces of large rocks. Rock phloxes, mossy saxifrages and *Polygonum affine* are ideal for this.

Where the original soil is unsuitable for a particular plant, take out a pocket and fill with a made-up soil mix. If the soil is predominantly limy, however, the sensible plan is to concentrate on chalk and limestone lovers, of which the choice is almost unlimited.

3 Make sure soil is worked down under and between rocks when planting up a crevice. A wooden rammer is an ideal tool.

4 Always remove weeds before planting rock plants. This encrusted saxifrage has creeping oxalis around the crown, one of the most difficult weeds to control.

1 Group the plants out over the bed and move them about to find the most suitable positions. Shade lovers need the protection of a large rock or place in gully.

2 Plant the dwarf shrubs first. These will be the 'trees' of your miniature mountain landscape. Well firm down soil round roots. This dwarf azalea will brighten a large rock next spring. Where plants require special conditions, take out a pocket of soil and refill with suitable compost mix. This gritty mix is ideal for the encrusted and kabschian saxifrages.

5 Small plants are best grouped to achieve a good show. Plant in threes or fives depending on the size of area and vigour of plants.

DECEMBER
Jobs for the month

A close watch must be kept on autumn-sown sweet peas throughout winter. They need cool conditions at present, but protection from rain and frost is necessary, so keep in a well-ventilated cold frame. Nip out the growing tips of those seedlings that so far have failed to produce side shoots naturally. They can be potted individually now. Lift the root system with as much compost as possible, taking care not to bruise the stems, and pot in plastic drinking cups with drainage holes. Watch out for pests such as aphids or small caterpillars, which will distort growing tips or chew up the foliage. Treat with an insecticidal dust like derris and keep in a well-lit cold frame, covered with sacking when hard frost is forecast.

Frosts will have blackened dahlia haulms in most districts by early December, so dig up tubers, clean away the soil, cut back the stems, carefully label and store in a frost-free place. After they have dried off and bruised or damaged portions been dusted with fungicide, place in boxes of peat, vermiculite or dry soil, spaced so they do not touch each other.

Germinating alpine plant seeds

Many beginners have trouble germinating seeds of alpine plants, but if they are sown now and kept moist and cold they should germinate well in spring. Keeping the seeds dry in a refrigerator is ideal for storing, but without moisture they cannot undergo the important vernalisation process, often essential for good germination.

2   Sow the seeds thinly and evenly over the compost surface by gentle tapping out of the packet or off your hand. Just cover with a little sieved compost.

3   Sprinkle a thin layer of fine grit over the surface. Putting some builders' sand through an old flour sieve will leave the ideal grit size. Place pans outside and protect them from rain with a sheet of glass. Make sure that the compost doesn't dry out in winter.

1   Take a small, well-crocked pot, add some coarse gravel or rough peat rubbings, fill almost to the rim with gritty compost, firm level and water.

Protecting plants from frosts

Frost will lift plants, especially newly planted ones, out of the ground. Cold winds are likely to kill off tender shoots, so provide winter protection.

1 Refirm plants that have been lifted out of the ground by frost or the roots will be seriously damaged. This is a common problem on peaty soils.

2 Where bulbs are showing tips of shoots above the soil, protect them from cold winds with small mounds of sand or weathered ashes.

3 Frost and rain will ruin any flowers that come during winter, so cover with small cloches.

4 Crowns of tender plants like crinums need some extra protection. Give them an overcoat of bracken or straw, secured by pegs and twine.

5 Tender climbing plants can be wrapped in straw or bracken held down with bird netting.

Vegetables

SOME LAYOUT HINTS

One good rule to follow when laying out the vegetable garden is to run all the rows north to south. This ensures that each side of each plant gets equal sunlight as the sun moves across the sky. Pick a sunny, sheltered spot for tomatoes, runner beans, soft fruit and early salad crops, although later salad sowings will prefer shade. Early peas and broad beans can also go into the warmest part of the plot.

Any area that is heavily shaded by trees or buildings will be best occupied by the compost heap or tool shed. Don't forget to leave room for a nursery bed for raising seedlings. Any rough areas that you do not have time to cultivate properly can be planted with potatoes. The root action helps to break up the soil and the heavy foliage discourages weeds.

Think about crop rotation right from the start by splitting the plot into three equal sections divided by paths. This has the added advantage that a far greater proportion of the ground can be reached and worked from a path without the need to step on the soil and thereby cause unnecessary compaction. You can also wheel barrows full of heavy manure, compost, etc, near to where you want to unload them.

Crop rotation

It has always been considered good practice to keep the different vegetable families on the move around the garden. There are several reasons for this, the most often quoted being that if the cabbage family is grown in the same place for long, a build-up of club-root disease is likely.

The possibility applies to other diseases too . . . the root fungus troubles of the onion and shallot family for instance, and fusarium in peas. But as well as disease, pests which attack one group in particular are encouraged by successive sowing or planting of the same crop, possibly the most destructive being eel-worm in potatoes.

There are other considerations too. The different groups get their food from the soil in different ways, and take it or leave it in different quantities. Shallow rooted subjects feed on the top 2–3in (5–7.5cm). Parsnips and carrots reach down into the bottom layers. Brussels sprouts and all the cabbage family drain the soil of nitrogen,

and peas and beans leave it behind after they've gone. The clever gardener takes advantage of all the plants' likes and dislikes.

And so the merry-go-round of crop rotation goes on. It may not be so practicable in the small garden as on the allotment, but the principles may always be borne in mind, and acted on as strictly as possible.

The families These are the families of vegetables:

Chenopodiaceae Beetroot, spinach.

Compositae Artichoke (globe and Jerusalem), lettuce.

Cruciferae Broccoli, brussels sprouts, cabbage, cauliflowers, kale, savoy, swede, turnip.

Cucurbitacae Cucumber, marrow.

Leguminosae Broad bean, french bean, runner bean, peas.

Liliaceae Asparagus, leek, onion, shallot.

Solanaceae Aubergine, capsicum, potato, tomato.

Umbelliferae Carrots, celery, parsley, parsnip.

Vegetables from the same group should not immediately follow each other in any rotation plan.

Rotation plan This is a suggested rotation plan for the main vegetables in the first year. Divide the plot into three sections and crop as follows.

Section 1 For root vegetables: carrots, parsnips, beetroot. No fresh manure. Anything added must be of a fine texture . . . peat, leafmould, mushroom compost, etc. Rake a balanced fertiliser into the surface a week or so before sowing the seeds.

Section 2 For the brassicas: cabbage, cauliflowers, brussels, etc, and for the peas and beans. Manure or compost dug in during the autumn. Limed in the winter, and a balanced fertiliser raked in during spring. Any ground vacant before or after a crop can be used for salads.

Section 3 For the potatoes, early and late. Any manure or compost dug in during autumn, or put in the trenches at planting time. No lime. Plant leeks when early potatoes are dug. Onions, seeds or sets, can go on this plot, or can be given a permanent bed.

In the second year, move the crops and plots round to read 3-1-2, and in the third year to 2-3-1.

A handful of delicious, tender turnips, the others having been left to grow bigger

JANUARY
Jobs for the month

Sowings in a heated greenhouse can include onions, leeks, tomatoes, french beans and radishes.

Outdoor beds can be dressed with lime if the soil is acid, but allow at least six weeks after manuring.

Dead or decaying leaves should be removed from winter lettuce as soon as they are noticed. If left, the rot will spread to the rest of the plant.

Preliminary work can begin on the onion bed. Give a dressing of bonemeal and bonfire ash if you have any.

Early-sown peas and broad bean seeds run the risk of being eaten by mice. Putting down poison could be dangerous to children, pets and birds, but a few traps set along the rows usually pay dividends.

Trenched celery should still be giving a succession of sticks for winter salads, but beware the depredations of slugs and severe weather. Put down slug pellets along the rows, covering with tiles or broken plant pots if pets roam the garden, and replace straw litter where wind has moved it away from the mound, adding more if severe frosts are forecast. Lift plants carefully to avoid damaging this valuable crop.

Get first peas in

Provided the ground isn't too wet or frozen to work, you can sow the first row or two of early round-seeded pea varieties like Feltham First and Meteor. They like ground that has been manured in autumn, but give a light dressing of a balanced fertiliser a week before sowing. Covering the site with cloches for a week or two before sowing will help to warm and dry the soil.

2 Sow a treble row of seeds, spacing them out 2–3in (5–7.5cm) each way.

3 Cover the seeds by drawing in the soil from the sides of the trench.

1 After breaking down large soil clods and raking the ground level, take out a shallow trench about 2–3in (5–7.5cm) deep with a draw hoe or spade.

4 Especially on heavy ground, it's best to firm down soil with the head of a rake at this time of year. This will avoid overcompacting the soil, which results in bad drainage. Early peas need the protection of frames and cloches to ward off the effects of cold winds and frosts.

Stored potatoes

It is always a good idea to check through stored potatoes as you use them and throw away all those showing signs of rot. Frost-free conditions are necessary to keep tubers sound, but temperatures above 40°F (4°C) will induce sprouting, which should not be allowed when tubers are to be grown on this year.

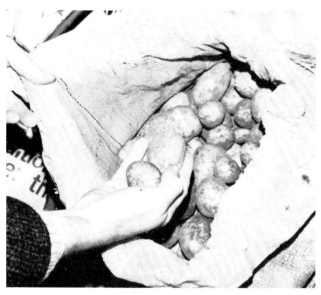

1   Periodically check potatoes in store and discard any that are not sound. If necessary, sort out the healthiest to grow on next year, but choose only disease-free ones.

3   Seed or once-grown tubers for growing on should be placed in boxes ready for chitting next month. Keep them in an airy but frost-free place until required.

2   Dry rot is a common disease. All those affected should be burned and handling of seed should be reduced to a minimum to avoid spreading the infection.

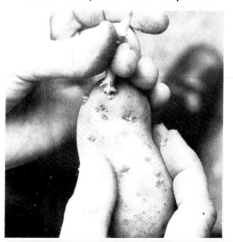

4   If seed tubers have already produced large sprouts, rub them out and reduce the temperature to at least 40°F (4°C). Most varieties will produce more sprouts from dormant eyes. If one or two tubers have been found infected with white rot or other disorders, dust the remainder with a fungicide to reduce the spread of the disease.

Early lettuce

Salad crops are at a premium during the winter and early spring, so keep a sharp watch on crops like lettuce that are now growing on the vegetable plot. Weeds and pests will still be lurking about, so take steps to keep them under control.

1 Periodically check the progress of lettuces under frames and cloches. Remove any weeds and treat the plants with an insecticidal dust if pests are seen. Control slugs with pellets.

2 Small seedling lettuce can be used to fill any gaps in the rows. These will mature later and provide a succession of salading.

3 We can expect a certain amount of fierce weather now, so secure polythene tunnels with soil on the side that receives the full force of the prevailing wind.

4 Where the ground is workable, the first sowing of lettuce seed can be made. Choose a sheltered, well-drained spot and work a general fertiliser into the soil.

5 Rake down the sowing site into a fairly fine tilth and sow thinly in short rows. If you find sowing difficult, try one of the proprietary seed sowers.

6 Cover the seeds and protect rows with small cloches or a portable frame. Watch out for slugs as the seedlings come through the soil.

FEBRUARY
Jobs for the month

Parsnips left in the ground should be lifted and stored in dry sand or peat before they begin to sprout again.

Outdoor plantings can include onion sets, shallots and chives.

Outdoor sowings of broad beans can be made now provided the ground is not frozen or waterlogged. If this is the case, they can be started off indoors in boxes or pots and planted out next month when conditions are more suitable. Sow in moist compost either individually in small pots or about 3in (7.5cm) apart in boxes, and cover with compost. Kept warm and moist, they will show through after about a week. Wait until two leaves are formed before planting into the garden.

Individual large tubers of Jerusalem artichokes or clumps of smaller ones can be planted from now until March. Take out a narrow trench or drill 4–6in (10–15cm) deep, work in a sprinkling of fertiliser or some well-rotted manure and space the tubers or clumps 15in (38cm) apart, discarding all which feel soft or are damaged. Fill in the trench and firm the soil with the flat part of a rake head.

Seed germination

Rates of seed germination are built-in characteristics. But soil temperatures come into it too. Because it's colder, March sowings will be slower than May ones, even from seeds taken from the same packet. That is why they come quicker in warm soils under cloches. Moisture is another governing factor. Seeds will lie dormant in the drills if there is not enough moisture to start off the germinating process. That is why it's so important to water the drills just before sprinkling in the seed.

Fresh seeds will germinate more quickly and surely than stale ones. If we keep seeds from one year to the other, we can expect them to get progressively slower and less sure to appear. There comes a time with most seeds when they are no longer worth sowing.

One other thing should be mentioned. It is possible for seeds to germinate and be lost before they are through the ground. They may be attacked just as they are coming through, or immediately they are through, by soil pests, slugs, caterpillars, birds, mice, drought or even strong sun. Watering and shaded cloches (if necessary) will take care of weather conditions and slug pellets and black cotton criss-crossed over the beds will deter some of the pests.

This table shows the average time taken for seeds to germinate in the open ground, assuming that they are fresh, and that there is sufficient warmth and moisture to get them started. It also shows the average life of seeds kept in cool, dry conditions, assuming that they are not in air-tight sealed packets.

Vegetable seed	Germinating time	Keeping time
Beans (all kinds)	7–14 days	3 years
Beetroot	10–18 days	6 years
Brassicas (all kinds)	5–10 days	5 years
Carrots	12–18 days	4 years
Chicory	5–10 days	8 years
Cucumbers (outdoor varieties)	7–14 days	6 years
Leeks	10–18 days	3 years
Lettuces	6–10 days	5 years
Marrows	7–14 days	6 years
Onions	10–16 days	3 years
Parsley	15–23 days	3 years
Parsnips	12–24 days	2 years
Peas	7–14 days	3 years
Radishes	3–6 days	5 years
Spinach	7–10 days	5 years

Sowing parsnips

Parsnips can go in during February if soil conditions allow, or if not, any time during March and even into early April. On well-worked, reasonably good soils, they can be sown thinly in shallow drills drawn 15–18in (38–45cm) apart. If your soil has proved unsuitable for this crop in the past, try preparing individual sowing stations of compost.

1 Rake down a plot of dug soil that was manured for a previous crop, after applying general fertiliser at the rate of 3oz per sq yd (90gm per sq m).

2 On soils that have proved unsuitable for root crops, prepare special planting positions with a crowbar at
10–12in (25–30cm) intervals.

3 Top up holes with good compost to about 1in (2.5cm) of
the soil surface.

4 Sow four or five seeds at
each of the special positions
and top up with more com-
post. Gently firm down.
Seedlings will later be
thinned to leave the strongest individual to grow on.

Preparing a runner bean trench

This is a good time to get the runner bean trench ready,
applying generous amounts of organic materials, especially on the quick-draining lighter soils. Don't firm
down, but allow the soil to settle naturally and remember,
radish seeds can be sown as a successional catch crop
until the beans go in.

1 Mark out the position of the trench and dig
out to a spade's depth and about 2ft (60cm)
wide. Next, add organic material like compost,
leaf mould or pulverised bark.

2 Thoroughly mix the organic material into the
second spit by forking. This will help to conserve moisture in summer on light soils and improve drainage on heavy grounds.

3 Fill the trench with the original soil, then rake
over to remove stones and level the surface
ready for sowing a crop of early radishes.

Starting shallots

As long as frost-free conditions can be maintained, you can start shallots into growth indoors early in the month, either individually in pots or spaced out in trays of well-drained compost. By rooting bulbs early, you can plant outside as soon as ground conditions are suitable, greatly reducing the risk of lifting by frost or birds.

3   Use plastic or wooden trays filled with compost, firming down so that the surface is about $\frac{1}{2}$in (13mm) from the rim to allow for adequate watering.

1   Sort through the bulbs and remove any loose outer scales that could attract moulds.

4   Push bulbs into the compost, spacing them evenly over the tray.

2   Damaged specimens should be discarded, as these may easily fall victim to infection and rot.

5   Give the trays a soaking, allow excess water to drain off and after that never allow them to dry out completely. Start them into growth in a frost-free greenhouse, but avoid high temperatures, or weak plants will result. If mould appears on the coat of a bulb, dust it with fungicide.

Chitting seed potatoes

From the middle of the month onwards you can begin to 'chit' seed potatoes to encourage strong shoot formation. Use top quality 'seed' tubers whenever possible, but if you're intending to use some of last year's crop, make sure they are sound.

1 Tubers about the size of a large hen's egg are ideal. Discard those showing signs of disease or damage.

2 If sprouting has already begun, rub out any that are damaged or white and drawn. Further sprouting will usually occur from other eyes.

3 Set the tubers, eyes up, in a tray, then put them in a good light and frost-free conditions. Sprouting will be rapid in warm places, so reduce the temperature to slow growth if necessary.

4 If more than one trayful is to be sprouted, boxes with corner pillars are useful. This allows stacking which saves space in small greenhouses or sheds.

5 Check the tubers periodically for signs of disease or aphids, but avoid excessive handling. Treat sprouts with insecticide if aphids are seen, but remove diseased tubers.

MARCH
Jobs for the month
Sowings this month can include parsnips, broccoli, summer spinach, spinach beet, sprouts, cabbage, cauliflower, early carrots, leeks, onions, lettuces, peas and radishes.

Broad beans can be sown in pots or boxes, or, as here, in plastic cups with a hole drilled through the bottom for drainage

Broad beans sown in heat last month will soon be ready for hardening off and planting out. If they were kept moist and in good light after germination they should have made strong sturdy plants like these, which were grown individually in plastic drinking cups. Plant 9in (23cm) apart in rows 18–24in (45–60cm) apart and water in.

Catch and inter-cropping
Getting the most from the vegetable plot means making provision for catch and inter-cropping as well as the overall rotation scheme. Catch crops are those that can be sown, grown and harvested in a short space of time, which makes it possible to put them in places where other crops are to be grown, or have been grown. Inter-crops are the same quick-maturing things set between rows of slow-growers. Lettuces and radishes are the quickest of all, but beetroots and carrots for pulling young are ideal fillers. The essence is to keep all of the ground occupied.

Runner beans aren't sown until mid-May, or planted until early June, and if a trench has been prepared in advance, there is time for radishes over the whole area, or lettuces, carrots or beetroot sown that they will be between or outside the actual bean stations. Early cabbage or cauliflower can also be set here. There is always fair space between rows of peas too or, if ground is allocated for them to be sown in May or June, it can be sown with salads in March and cleared by pea sowing time.

A good example of inter-cropping: a quick crop of radish growing between two rows of potatoes, while, on the right, lettuces have been squeezed in between the potatoes and the path

Planting onion sets that were started off indoors in February

The ground in and around celery trenches is also vacant long enough to take a quick crop. Outdoor cucumbers and marrows need generous spacing and if the sites for these are prepared, and a stick put in to mark them, the ground between can be used until July at least.

There is also the less-obvious method of planting slow-growers between the quick. An example of this is cabbage, cauliflower and even brussels plants set between rows of half-grown lettuce or carrots and beetroot soon to be pulled. The timing must be such that the crops will be used before the brassica leaves spread and interfere with growth.

Finally, for quick-maturing crops, be sure to choose the right varieties. May Queen and Little Gem lettuces, Cherry Belle or Saxerre radishes, Early Nantes carrots and Boltardy beetroot are good choices.

Planting out shallots and onions

Shallots and onion sets should be planted at the earliest opportunity to allow a long growing season. Root growth, frost and birds will tend to unearth them, so unless you started them into growth in boxes indoors last month, bury them up to the neck to avoid constant refirming. Those started off need not be planted so deep as they will already have a good root anchorage. Break down well-dug soil that was manured in winter and rake level after applying a general balanced fertiliser. Firm down soil by rolling or gently treading and take out shallow drills spaced 12in (30cm) apart. Plant shallots at 6in (15cm) and onions at 9in (23cm) intervals by gently pushing into the soil. Push the soil up round the bulbs by hand and firm down. Where birds are troublesome in scratching out bulbs, cover the rows with strands of cotton or twine. Check periodically for frost lift and refirm immediately.

Sowing outside without using glass

The vegetable gardener who has only an open patch—no greenhouse, frames or cloches—can feel a bit frustrated at this time of the year when he reads about making an early start with sowings under glass. But glass is by no means essential for most things. Many vegetables will give good and perfectly satisfactory crops from seeds sown outside.

Note carefully the sowing dates. Where March is indicated, seeds go in as soon as the ground is dry enough on top. If it isn't possible to sow in March, sow at the first opportunity afterwards.

Leaf vegetables

	Sow seeds	Set plants	Distance between rows	Distance between plants	Harvest	Remarks
Brussels sprouts	March/April $\frac{1}{2}$in (13mm) deep in short drill for transplanting	May/June, can be bought at this time if seeds not sown	2–3ft (60–90cm)	2–3ft (60–90cm)	October to April	Needs good ground and firm planting
Cabbage						
Summer	March/April	May/June	18in (45cm)	15in (38cm)	July to October	Check varieties for
Winter	May	June/July	2ft (60cm)	2ft (60cm)	October to March	different sowing
Spring	July/August as for brussels	September/October as for brussels	18in (45cm)	9–18in (23–45cm)	March to May	and planting times
Cauliflower						
Summer	March/April	May/June	18in (45cm)	18in (45cm)	July to October	Must have good
Winter	May as above	June/July as above	2ft (60cm)	2ft (60cm)	March to June	conditions and no checks
Calabrese	March/April as above	May/June as above	18in (45cm)	18in (45cm)	August to November	Shoots must be continually picked; good for freezing
Sprouting broccoli	May as above	June/July as above	2ft (60cm)	2ft (60cm)	March to May	On the ground for a long time for such a short picking
Lettuce						
Summer	March/July at intervals for succession $\frac{1}{2}$in (13mm) deep	March/May plants taken from seed rows; early plants can be bought	12in (30cm)	6–9in (15–23cm)	May to October	Thinnings from rows can be transplanted until June; must have space and full light to heart up
Winter	August/September		12in (30cm)	9in (23cm)	April to May	
Spinach						
Summer	April/May/June		12in (30cm)	6in (15cm)	June to August	Summer varieties must
Winter	July/August		15in (38cm)	6in (15cm)	October to April	be used quickly
Leeks	March/April $\frac{1}{2}$in (13mm) deep in short drill for transplanting	Drop plants into 9in (23cm) deep holes when as thick as pencil; plants can be bought	18in (45cm)	9in (23cm)	November to April	Leave in ground all winter and dig as needed

Root vegetables

	Sow seeds	Between rows	Treatment	Harvest	Remarks
Beetroot	April/July 1–1$\frac{1}{2}$in (2.5–4cm) deep	12–15in (30–38cm)	First thin seedlings to 3in (7.5cm) apart, then continue thinning when roots big enough to use	July to October	Will store in sand from October–April; April/May sowings best used in summer
Carrots	March/July 1in (2.5cm) deep	12in (30cm)	Pull and use early and late sowings as needed; May sowing thin to 4in (10cm) for storing	June to October	Use soil insecticide to deter carrot fly; store as beetroot
Parsnips	March/April 1in (2.5cm) deep	15in (38cm)	Thin seedlings to 6–8in (15–20cm) apart	October to April	Leave in ground to dig as needed
Turnips	March/July 1in (2.5cm) deep	12in (30cm)	Thin seedlings to 4–6in (10–15cm); pull and use when roots big enough	June to March	Dust insecticide on seedlings to deter flea beetle; store as beet and carrots
Onions					
Salad	March/June $\frac{1}{2}$in (13mm)	10in (26cm)	Pull as needed; thin out seedlings to 4in (10cm)	June to October	Two sowings will give
Bulb	March/April 1in (2.5cm) deep	12in (30cm)		September	continuous supply of salads; bulbs for storing must be well
Japanese	August 1in (2.5cm) deep	12in (30cm)	Thin out March/April	June to December	harvested with the tops dried off
Sets	March/April	12in (30cm)	Plant bulbs half buried 6in (15cm) apart	September	naturally; need good soil
Radish	March/July 1in (2.5cm) deep	9in (23cm)	Pull as soon as big enough; sow at three-week intervals for continuous supply	May to September	Quick to grow and can be used as catch crop; deter flea beetle as for turnip

Peas and beans

	Sow seeds	Distance between rows	Distance between plants	Treatment	Remarks
Broad beans	March, 4in (10cm) apart	2–3ft (60–90cm)		Pinch off tips above top flower to deter black fly; spray if necessary	Must be picked regularly as pods develop
Dwarf beans	May/July, 2in (5cm) deep, 3in (7.5cm) apart	18in (45cm)	Thin to 6in (15cm)	May need slight support in windy situations	Pick regularly; three sowings will give continuous supply from July onwards
Runner beans	Mid to late May, 2in (5cm) deep	Single rows 4ft (1.2m), double 6ft (1.8m)	10in (26cm)	Need rich ground and plenty of moisture; overhead sprayings will help 'set' flowers; need good support, 6ft (1.8m) or more high	Sow a few seeds into pots or boxes to fill gaps if necessary; must be picked regularly
Peas	March/June; space seeds 2in (5cm) apart and 2in (5cm) deep	18in–4ft (45cm–1.2m) depending on height of the variety		Varieties over 18in (45cm) must be supported, all are better for support; protect from birds	Sow early varieties in March and June, maincrop varieties in April and May; pick regularly

After transplanting brassicas, water well and keep the rows watered until the plants are established

Use the back of your spade or shovel to firm the soil down to form a ridge along your rows of celery. Spray plants with malathion if you notice any signs of celery fly and with Bordeaux mixture to prevent leaf spot disease

Starting celery from seed

Where indoor heat is available, both trench and self-blanching celery can be started from seed early in the month. They will be ready for planting out in June.

1 Fill a seed tray with well-drained compost and firm level to within ½in (13mm) of the rim.

2 Soak well with a fine rose and allow to drain.

3 Sprinkle the seeds evenly over the compost. You can sow small quantities of both sorts at the same time, making sure they are separated and clearly labelled to avoid confusion later.

4 Cover seeds with fine compost and gently firm down. Further watering should be unnecessary until seedlings appear.

5 Cover the tray with glass and shade with paper until seeds germinate. It's a good idea to wipe off each day any condensation that forms on the glass. Once the seedlings are large enough to handle, prick them out into a rich compost.

APRIL
Jobs for the month

Plants of all kinds of cabbages, cauliflowers, brussels, etc, can be bought now ready to set out in May and June. Or seeds can still be sown. Sow in ½in (13mm) drills and transplant when 6in (15cm) high. The smallest packet of seed will produce between 50 and 100 plants.

Peas never go less than 2ft (60cm) apart, with more space for tall varieties. For succession continue sowing 2–3in (5–7.5cm) deep with seeds about 1in (2.5cm) apart. Mice and birds are the pests to guard against.

Onions for pulling young as salads are best sown separate from those sown for keeping. White Lisbon is the best variety and can be sown two or three times for succession.

Lettuces are the mainstay of salads and should be sown every three weeks or so. Sow very thinly about ½in (13mm) deep, in rows 9–12in (23–30cm) apart. Plants raised in greenhouses and frames can be set out and will need protection from slugs and birds.

Carrots for pulling young are best sown separate from the maincrop. Sow early varieties now, with the maincrop in May.

Beetroot are inclined to bolt (go to seed) if sown too early. Boltardy can be risked now for early pull, but the main sowing should be in May.

In colder districts it is still worth putting cloches over newly set out plants and early sowings. French beans can be sown under cloches, but not too many—there's still a risk.

This is a good time to make a new mint bed. If the old bed is weedy, dig up some young outside roots and replant them in a new position.

Sow parsley in ½in (13mm) deep drills in a convenient spot for picking. It may take six to eight weeks to germinate. Sow fairly thickly, but thin plants out to 3–4in (7.5–10cm) apart.

Cut any flower heads from rhubarb as soon as they can be recognised. Take off any forcing covers that may have been used as soon as outside sticks are available. Sprinkle a balanced fertiliser round each root and hoe in.

Sow sweet corn indoors, two or three to a small pot and thinned out to the best seedling. After hardening off, plant out in early June.

Soil and weather conditions permitting, gardeners in mild districts can begin sowing runner beans outside in the middle of the month—but they will need the protection of cloches early on in case of frost. Sow 3in (7.5cm) deep in double rows spaced 12in (30cm) apart. Allow 6in (15cm) between each seed. In cold districts it's best to sow indoors in boxes or individually in small plastic cups with drainage holes punched in them Germinate at 50–55°F (10–13°C) and plant out at the two-leaf stage.

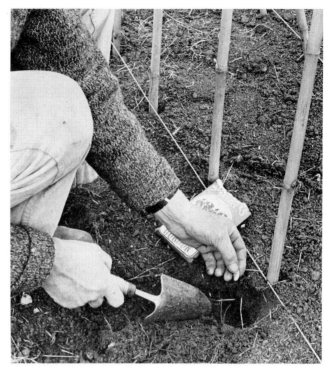

To avoid disturbing the roots of runner beans later on, it is a good idea to erect the supporting frame before sowing. You can also ensure that there is a plant at every pole

Radishes are probably the easiest and earliest maturing salad crop to grow from seed. Only small amounts need be sown at one time, so one packet should be sufficient to sow every fortnight or so from March onwards to give a succession of roots well into summer. In March, and if the weather is on the cold side in early April, sow in a cold frame or under cloches. Otherwise choose a well-drained, sunny spot, adding a general fertiliser a week or more beforehand.

After raking soil down into a fine tilth, take out shallow drills 6in (15cm) apart and sow seeds thinly. Cover the drills by carefully drawing soil in with your rake across the rows.

Sowing brassica seeds

An unused corner can usually be found for a few short rows of brassicas. Prepare a seed bed by either raking to a fine tilth or working in some seedling compost. An easy way to make the ½in (13mm) drills is to press a cane lightly into the previously watered soil. Sow the seeds fairly thinly, cover with soil and protect with a cloche if possible. Always label the rows carefully because all brassica seedlings look the same to the inexperienced eye.

Get maincrop potatoes in

By the middle of the month the maincrop potatoes can be planted. This crop is a heavy feeder, so add plenty of organic material to the base of the planting drills and also apply artificials when you fill in. Apart from its richness and moisture-retaining properties, a good lining of humus will also help to prevent scab on the tubers.

1 A nice tray of seed potatoes, which are the right size—as big as a duck egg—and have been chitted to perfection with clusters of sturdy ½–1in (13mm–2.5cm) shoots at the rose end.

2 This plot has had a lot of rotted straw rotovated in to improve its water-holding capacity. A trench 6in (15cm) has been dug and the bottom lined with old, ripe manure.

3 Maincrop varieties such as King Edward, Pentland Crown and Desiree can be planted, shoots uppermost, 12–15in (30–38cm) apart in the rows, which should be 24–30in (60–75cm) apart.

4 Just cover the tubers with infill soil and then sprinkle a balanced granular fertiliser along the row before completely filling the row and leaving the soil slightly mounded. Another sprinkling of fertiliser can be given when the shoots show through.

Opposite

Above Of all late summer bedding flowers, dahlias are probably the most spectacular and give the best results, coming as they do in many colours, forms and heights. *Below* Dahlias are grown from fleshy corms, cuttings or from seeds; this is a fine bed of seedlings.

MAY

Jobs for the month

Individual sites for marrows and cucumbers can be prepared. Dig out the top spit of soil 1yd (90cm) square, turn manure, compost or something similar into the next spit down and replace the top soil, mixing it with peat and a sprinkling of general fertiliser. Mark the spot with a stick in the centre and leave to settle before planting next month. Much the same preparations can be made for tomatoes, aubergines and peppers, remembering that they need warm, sunny spots, protected from the wind.

Sprinkle calomel dust around onion, cabbage and carrot seedlings.

As soon as the spring greens have finished, clear away the remains so that they don't provide a home for pests.

Don't let weeds get started

There is an old gardening adage that 'one year's seeds means seven years' weeds'. This is true unfortunately, and is one good reason why the hoe should be in constant use at this time of the year. Another value of regular hoeing between the rows is that the soil surface is continually being worked and broken up, keeping it open and moisture-receptive.

Never allow weeds to grow and seed—which they do very quickly—because the seeds can remain dormant in the soil for many years, even if deeply dug in. When a subsequent digging brings them nearer the surface, they germinate and the whole vicious circle starts all over again.

A few minutes spent regularly with a Dutch hoe when the sun is shining will save hours of toil in later weeks, months and even years. Dutch hoeing has two functions: it leaves seedlings on top of the ground with roots exposed to killing sun and winds, and also deprives perennial weeds of their leaves. However persistent they are through their underground spreading roots, no weed can live for ever without making leaves.

The difference between a Dutch hoe and other types is that it is used working backwards. This means that you don't have to walk on hoed ground and probably tread weeds back into the soil, where they will root again. It is important not to dig in too deeply with the blade. It should be at such an angle that, when held in a comfortable working position, the blade slides horizontally just beneath the surface.

Use a Dutch hoe at an angle so that the blade slides just under the surface

Transplanting brassicas

Brussels sprouts need a firm site if they are to button up. When pulling transplants of any members of the brassica family from a seed bed, water well the night before lifting. Apply a general fertiliser to the site, rake in, tread the ground firm if for brussels and make shallow drills about 2½ft (75cm) apart for brussels or between 1½–2ft (45–60cm) for others. To prevent club-root and root fly, shake calomel dust into the planting hole. Space plants about the same distance apart in the rows as the distance between rows. Well firm in, water and keep moist.

Before transplanting any members of the brassica family, dip the roots into a paste of calomel dust, or shake the dry dust into the hole.

Opposite

Above Like the closely related azaleas, rhododendrons do not generally like a limestone soil, but if lime is a problem you can still enjoy these lovely shrubs by planting them in raised beds containing a more acid compost. *Below* A close up of the beautiful bell-shaped rhododendron flower.

Sowing sweet corn, marrows and runner beans

Sweet corn, marrows, cucumbers and runner beans can either be sown in pots or boxes in a greenhouse, cold frame or even indoors early in the month, to be planted out later, or sown directly outside towards the end of the month. Modern F1 hybrids of sweet corn are more suited to our climate, so try early-maturing varieties like First of All and Earliking, or taller, later types such as Kelvedon Glory or North Star. They all like a sunny, sheltered position.

If you are sowing direct, apply a general fertiliser and rake into the ground. Sweet corn should be block sown or planted as it is wind-pollinated. Draw out short drills spaced 18–24in (45–60cm) apart and 1in (2.5cm) deep. Sow seeds in pairs at 15–18in (38–45cm) intervals and later take out the weakest seedlings. Cover the seeds with soil, gently firm and water if the ground is dry.

If you are starting plants under cover, the seeds can go into boxes 2–3in (5–7.5cm) apart or in individual pots. Almost any compost will do.

1   Sow two or even three seeds to a pot as an insurance against poor germination.

2   If they all grow, remove all but the strongest plant in each pot.

3   Plant out to the same spacing as directly-sown plants, taking out a planting hole with a trowel and well firming afterwards.

Take out drills 2in (5cm) deep, water and sow dwarf beans at 6in (15cm) intervals

Sow dwarf beans

Dwarf beans, which are particularly valuable in a dry summer, can be sown now. They like a warm soil, so in cold districts it pays to cloche the site a week or two before sowing, and then until the plants are through. Ground manured the previous winter is best. Apply a balanced fertiliser, rake the soil fine and take out drills 2in (5cm) deep and about 18in (45cm) apart if more than one row is needed.

If the soil is dry, water the drills before sowing at 6in (15cm) intervals. Sow some extra at the ends of the rows to fill any gaps later on. Cover with soil and lightly firm.

Among root crops needing a general feed now are carrots

JUNE
Jobs for the month

Harvesting of earlier sown crops will have begun in earnest, but there is still much sowing to be done. Continue with salad crops in short rows for succession. Carrots and beetroot can still go in too, as can turnips and swedes, and up to mid-month there is still time for a final sowing of peas and broad beans. This is also dwarf and runner bean sowing time if you have not already raised plants indoors. Winter and spring cabbages can still be sown, for transplanting into position later.

Autumn- and winter-maturing brassica seedlings from earlier sowings can be planted out. These include brussels sprouts, cabbage, savoys and sprouting broccoli. Like winter cauliflower, brussels like a firm soil, so there's no need to dig. Just hoe in a fertiliser and remove persistent weeds.

General maintenance work includes regular weeding and watering.

When earthing up potatoes, remember that other plants will benefit from this treatment too. Pulling soil up around the stems of early cauliflowers and other greens with a hoe will not only prevent wind rock but will discourage the cabbage root fly from laying its egs. Peas will respond to earthing by making new roots from the base of the stem and cropping more vigorously. Do this just before putting in the supports.

Many culinary herbs are ready for harvesting and drying. Chervil and dill can be sown now.

There should be little, if any empty ground because at this time of year every square inch of precious soil should be put to work. Even odd little corners should be filled with salad crops such as lettuce and radish.

Outdoor ridge cucumber plants raised earlier must have been hardened off before putting out. Seeds can still be sown on the mounds early in the month for late cropping. Sow about 1in (2.5cm) deep in small groups and thin later to leave only the strongest seedlings.

Some of the more vigorous crops that are on the way to maturity will benefit from another application of a general fertiliser to boost growth. Potatoes could do with 4oz per sq yd (120gm per sq m) as could beetroot, other root crops and spinach.

Keep potatoes growing strongly and healthily by regular hoeing and spraying when necessary to control pests like aphids and other sucking insects. Slugs can be reduced by putting down pellets or spraying ground with metaldehyde.

Outdoor tomatoes that have been raised in a cold greenhouse or frame can be planted out up to the end of the month. Standard varieties like Outdoor Girl, Moneymaker and Gardener's Delight will need staking, although bush types like Pixie, The Amateur and French Cross do not. Leave side shoots on bush tomatoes.

To help shallots to ripen by next month, carefully scrape away the soil from around the clusters of bulbs to allow the sun to get at them.

Bush tomato Pixie in a growing bag outside on a patio

Plant celery

An important job this month is planting hardened-off celery into prepared sites. White-stemmed varieties such as Fenlander will eventually require earthing up, so plant in a trench of rich soil that has preferably been prepared earlier and left so that the infill soil is 3in (7.5cm) lower than ground level. This crop is normally planted in double rows about 12in (30cm) apart, leaving 10in (26cm) between plants, but for moderate supplies you can put them out in a single row. Self-blanching types such as Avonpearl are planted in half-rows, allowing 9in (23cm) between plants. It is important to keep celery well supplied with water, and if brown patches appear on the leaves or stems, dust or spray the plants with Bordeaux mixture, as this is a symptom of leaf spot disease.

It's turnip time

The earliest turnips, sown in late March, should be maturing by the end of the month. Continuous sowings can be made up until the end of July to give a succession of crops. Sow $\frac{3}{4}$in (2cm) deep in drills drawn 12–15in (30–38cm) apart, thin progressively to 6–9in (15–23cm) and allow about three months from seed to maturity.

If you have not had much previous success with self-blanching celery, a good variety to try is Carter's Golden Self Blanching.

1   If desired, seedlings can be thinned to their final spacing as soon as they are large enough to handle. Note the use of the plank to avoid soil compaction.

2   A more profitable way is to thin progressively so that turnips are large enough at the final thinning to provide tasty, half-mature roots.

Don't be afraid to 'bury' leeks

Leeks will be in the ground for a long time, so the wise gardener puts them to one side of the plot, so that they are not in the way of autumn clearing and digging. There are several methods of planting, but dropping them in holes—the deeper the hole the greater the length of blanch—is a good one. The bed should previously have been enriched with plenty of manure dug well down. Select the thickest seedlings—pencil size is ideal—trim the roots to half-length and cut the tops so that all the plants are the same length.

1   Having firmed the bed with the feet, lay down a garden line and make planting holes as deep as the plants are long on alternate sides every 6in (15cm). Use a thick cane to make the holes and mark the depth it needs to go in with a piece of string or a plant tie.

2   Drop a leek seedling into each hole—it was to make this easier that the roots were trimmed. Don't be worried if the tops barely show above ground—they will grow in a matter of days. Leave the holes open.

3   Fill the holes with water and repeat two days later. This has the effect of washing some soil down around the roots.

4   The same leeks only a month later. The stems have started to thicken up and foliage is about 6in (15cm) high.

JULY
Jobs for the month

Summer cabbage such us Golden Acre, which were transplanted in April and May, will be ready and can be cut as required. If you have too many at any one time, don't forget that cabbage can be frozen.

Onions should be bulbing up nicely. To encourage ripening, carefully scrape away the soil from around the bulbs, to allow the sun to get at them.

Leeks can be given a boost by watering the rows with a solution of sulphate of ammonia, $\frac{1}{2}$oz (14gm) per gallon (4.5 litres) of water.

Other crops that will appreciate a similar feed include beetroot, savoys, cabbages and cauliflowers. If using the granular form of sulphate of ammonia, make sure it doesn't touch the plants. Carefully sprinkle around the root area.

Many people don't realise that it's possible to transplant beetroot seedlings that have been thinned out. This is not normally possible with root crops, but beet are the exception to the rule. Remove the unwanted seedlings very carefully, ensuring that the tap root is undamaged, replant immediately in an adjoining row and water well and often until they settle down. Having suffered a severe check, the 'free' row will mature later than the first, giving a succession of roots.

Shallots should be ready for harvesting now. Lift carefully when the foliage yellows and begins to die down, separate the clusters of bulbs and remove soil from the roots, then lay them out in the sun to dry.

All cucurbits such as marrows, courgettes and ridge cucumbers will benefit from a weekly high potash feed and large amounts of water. When the shoots of trailing types of marrows have reached 3ft (90cm) they should have the tip pinched out to promote growth of side shoots.

Give all brassicas a weekly derris spray against caterpillars and aphis. As these pests tend to get into the curls of leaves, where sprays and birds can't reach them, you may prefer a systemic insecticide. Celery should also be sprayed against fly.

During long spells of hot, dry weather there is considerable moisture loss through the leaves of plants (transpiration) and evaporation from the soil, which will dry out almost as quickly as you can water it. The best method of moisture conservation is by mulching. This involves putting a 2in (5cm) or so layer of organic material such as garden compost, manure, peat, straw or grass clippings from the lawn (provided the grass has not recently been treated with selective weedkiller) around the plants, but not quite touching the stems. Give the ground a really good soaking first and the moisture will remain around the roots, where it is most needed, for a long time. Mulching is especially valuable in long gardens or on allotments where the nearest water supply is some distance away. Crops that will benefit include runner beans, celery, sweet corn and tomatoes.

Outdoor tomatoes can be fed when the first fruits have set and the side shoots (apart from the bush types) periodically nipped out. Leaves can be removed from around any ripening fruit. Canes and ties are the best method of supporting the upright types of tomatoes growing outside.

From mid-July to mid-August is the time to sow spring cabbage to give transplants during September and October. In the South, delay sowing until next month. Try Wheeler's Imperial if you have only a small plot, and Durham Elf, Golden Acre and Early Offenham.

A nice root of early potatoes. What will go into the ground next? *(Photo* Brian Furner)

Dig early potatoes and re-use ground

One of the reasons why potatoes are so useful for clearing rough ground is that the earth has to be worked three times during the growing process. The first time is the digging at planting time, the second is the hoeing and earthing up of the plants and the third is when the crop is dug. By now the gardener will be well into lifting his early spuds and it is essential that he cleans up the ground as he goes, especially as he will want to use the vacant ground for other crops.

What crops can replace the potatoes? Leeks or green-stuff are likely candidates, but remember that the winter brassicas and leeks will occupy the ground until next April or May and will interfere with winter digging. Late savoys and late cabbage, which come off in autumn and early winter, are a better bet.

If the ground can be broken fine enough to take seeds, there are many possibilities. Lettuce for autumn cutting can be sown in July—a variety like All the Year Round is ideal. Winter varieties like Arctic King can be sown in August, for cutting in early spring. The new Japanese onions have to be sown in August, or there is perpetual spinach or chicory. Even carrots, turnips, swedes and beetroot can go in and have time to make tender young roots by Christmas.

Successional carrots

Carrots will need thinning out to get good-sized roots, but remember any soil disturbance or the odour of crushed foliage is likely to attract the female carrot flies which are only too willing to lay their eggs. These hatch out into small grubs which bore into the roots.

1   Hoe between rows but hand weed in the rows to avoid soil disturbance. Once the plants have foliage about 2in (5cm) high, thin to $\frac{1}{2}$in (13mm) between bulk crop carrots, but for large roots thin in three stages to allow a final spacing of 4in (10cm) between plants. Thin after sunset.

2   Feed periodically by sprinkling a general fertiliser along the rows and water in. Applying BHC dust to the seedling rows (after watering) will help deter carrot root flies. The row being watered has been thinned to grow on as a main crop, while the one on the left will be thinned when the roots are 'finger' sized and can be eaten. The stone cat? He makes an effective bird scarer.

Look after your peas

Fresh garden peas are one of the most appetising of crops, but unless you give them regular care, crops will either be light or ruined by pea moth maggots. Giving the plants a lot of moisture is also important. The best time to water is as the pods are forming. A good soaking then can double the weight of crop.

Mulching the rows with rotted manure, compost or moist peat will help to conserve soil moisture during the summer. Apply after watering. Ten days after flowers open, spray thoroughly with an insecticide, with a repeat application a fortnight later. This will control the pea moth, which lays its eggs on the developing pods.

A fine row of Suttons' Chieftan peas

AUGUST
Jobs for the month

High winds can cause havoc among taller growing brassicas, so to avoid toppling, earth up the stems of kale and brussels sprouts, which are especially vulnerable. Maturing heads of cauliflowers can be discoloured by hot sun, so provide some protection by shading with a leaf broken over the curds, or tie up foliage.

Turnips sown early in the month will provide roots for immediate use or for storing from mid-October. Those sown late in the month will give a fine crop of leaves.

As soon as the tall foliage of onions begins to flop, the ripening process has started and you should bend over all those tops that will give without snapping. Leave those that won't bend and try again a few days later. It looks neater if all the tops are bent the same way. Once the bulbs have fully ripened they can be lifted ready for use or for storing. Harvest in either August or September, according to variety and weather conditions. For harvesting and storing see page 98.

The first half of the month is the best time to sow seeds of spring cabbage. Good varieties are Durham Elf, Flower of Spring, Wheelers Imperial and Avoncrest.

When stopping tomatoes always leave at least one leaf above the last truss (*Photo* T F Rice)

Outdoor tomatoes should be 'stopped'—nip out the growing tip so that the production of more stem leaves and trusses is stopped. The saved energy goes, instead, into the existing fruit. There is no fixed time for doing this, but normally by the middle of the month there is little point in allowing plants to go on making growth that will not have time to produce mature fruits. When the tip is pinched out, one leaf at least above the last truss must be left to go on drawing up the energy.

If you're going away on holiday

The garden can't take a holiday, even if you can, and everything will keep growing, weeds and all, or not do very well, depending upon how thoroughly you have prepared for your week or fortnight at the seaside.

Weeding is especially important as what are tiny seedlings now will have become a jungle in two weeks' time, so get the hoe working.

Young marrows developing behind the female flower

Before you leave for your holiday, make sure everything has a good soaking, especially thirsty crops like tomatoes, marrows, ridge cucumbers and celery, and put down a mulch if you have not already done so. If possible, try to get a friend to have a look at the plot while you are away. It pays to let someone harvest mature crops as this will encourage fresh flushes for your return.

Thin out seedlings like swedes, carrots, beetroots and lettuces to prevent overcrowding, which will result in plants competing against each other for water and nutrients. Swedes need a minimum spacing of at least 6in (15cm), beetroots 4in (10cm), carrots ½in (13mm) and lettuce 12in (30cm).

If the runner beans have reached the top of their frames, nip out the growing shoot to stop growth. Also make sure they are free of blackfly—spray promptly with insecticide to prevent a quick build-up of these damaging pests. Check all other crops for signs of pests and treat accordingly. Flea beetle (turnip fly) will be at work on turnips, radishes and swedes if the weather is dry and plants may need dusting with sevin or BHC preparations.

French beans are a most valuable crop, especially in a drought when runner beans may not have fared well

Drying or freezing herbs

Herbs of all kinds can be harvested now for drying or freezing. Shrubby types dry easily provided you hang them where moisture cannot start rotting, but freezer owners may like to lay down a store of the annual and soft perennial types.

1 Collect savoury herbs for storing, preferably when the foliage is dry and conditions are sunny. Harvest current year's growth on shrubby types like rosemary.

2 Lay stems on a wire hammock or tie in small bundles and hang up in a dry and airy place like the garage or loft. To retain maximum flavour it's essential to dry off gradually.

3 Herbs with soft growth like mint, dill, etc, can be frozen if required. Wash the leaves thoroughly to remove any insects or dirt.

4 Well dry the stems after washing and remove any faded or blemished leaves.

5 Coarse-leaved forms of mint are more easily handled when leaves are stripped and packed into covered containers. Slender herbs can be packed as succulent shoot tips.

6 Whole leaves or tips can be left as they are, or once frozen, they can be removed and pre-crumbled before covering container and returning it to the freezer.

SEPTEMBER
Jobs for the month

To get lettuces for winter salads, seedlings must be transplanted under the protection of cloches and frames. Where protection is not possible, sow winter varieties now into shallow drills spaced 12in (30cm) apart. Thin to 3in (7.5cm) apart, then again in stages during early spring to allow 9–12in (23–30cm) between maturing plants. With seedlings available now, plant in two rows, allowing 12in (30cm) each way for under cloches and give 8½in (21.5cm) spacing for cold frames. Put down slug pellets.

Watch out for signs of mildew on growing turnips and swedes. Treat with Dithane or Bordeaux mixture.

If the weather is hot, spray celery with Bordeaux mixture against leaf spot disease.

Gradually earth-up celery—not the self-blanching types, of course.

Earthing celery

Celery will need earthing up in stages once the plants have reached 12in (30cm) high. Don't ridge them up too much at first, but the second and third earthings can be heavier. The important thing is to prevent soil from falling into the heart by providing a collar or tying the stems in.

Before beginning to earth, check plants for suckers, which develop at the base. Remove by hand. Use the back of your spade or shovel to firm the soil down to form a ridge along the rows. Spray plants with malathion if celery fly is spotted and with Bordeaux mixture to prevent leaf spot disease.

Tie the stems together just below the leaves and wrap each plant in a collar of brown paper, polythene or PVC tubing. If the soil is dry, give the plants a thorough watering before filling in the trench with friable soil.

Harvesting potatoes

Successful storage of maincrop potatoes depends on how you lift them. Try to avoid bruising the tubers unduly and take out any damaged or diseased ones. Allow skins to harden in the sun, remove all soil and, if you haven't room to make a clamp outside, store in woven sacks that 'breathe'.

1 Cut the haulms down first, then lift the tubers carefully with a fork. Burn the stem and roots and allow the potatoes to dry for a couple of hours in the sun.

2 When the skins have hardened off, sort through them and weed out any that have been split during lifting and use these now. Discard the old seed tubers.

Harvest and store onions

Onion bulbs should be ready to lift and store two weeks after you have bent the tops over. Lay them on the ground or on wire hammocks to dry off fully before storing and discard all those that show any sign of damage.

1 Where onions have died off after the tops have been bent over, carefully lift them with a fork and lay on the ground to dry.

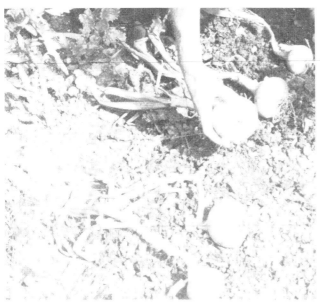

2 Once dried, check over crops for any showing signs of disease or damage. Burn soft, diseased bulbs and use any damaged ones immediately.

3 Lay bulbs in a sunny, dry spot to ripen off completely, then remove the shrivelled remains of foliage and loose outer scales.

4 Carefully cut off root remains with scissors and either make up an onion string (leave a fair length of neck for this) or store in net bags in a cool, dry and airy place.

OCTOBER
Jobs for the month

If you have a frame, cloche or greenhouse maintain a succession of spring lettuces by sowing small amounts of seed at intervals from now until March. Varieties include Dandie, May Queen, Kloek and Kwiek.

Gardeners in the north should plant out spring cabbage early in the month, but those further south can wait until mid-month. Plant 9in (23cm) apart with 18in (45cm) between rows, treating the roots to calomel dust or slurry against club-root. Although they will not need a fertiliser now, they will need a boost to growth next March in the form of nitrate of soda or sulphate of ammonia.

Protect the remaining self-blanching celery by putting down straw or bracken.

Protect autumn cauliflowers from frost by breaking a leaf over the curd.

Cauliflowers of the autumn heading varieties will be ready for cutting

Carrots sown before July can be stored in boxes of dry peat or sand, in sacks that allow good aeration, or by piling them against a wall and covering with a good layer of sand to make a clamp

Keeping vegetables during winter

Crops best left in their growing positions and gathered when needed include: Jerusalem artichokes (September–February); brussels sprouts (October–March); cabbage—late savoy and January King (November–March); blanched celery (October–January); leeks (November–April); parsnips (September–April); swedes and turnips (October–March).

Best harvested and stored through winter are: beetroot, carrots, celeriac, and swedes and turnips (in cold areas)—in containers of peat or sand or piled against a wall or fence and covered with 6in (15cm) of sand; winter-keeping cabbage—cut and keep in a cold outhouse; onions and shallots—after ripening, store in nets in an outhouse; potatoes—in sacks in a dark, frostproof but cool place.

NOVEMBER
Jobs for the month

Make the final earthing of trenched celery, taking care not to allow any soil to fall in the crowns or collars.

Keep brassica crops like purple sprouting broccoli clear of yellowing leaves and spray with insecticide if aphid or whitefly are spotted.

Broad beans sown outside early in the month will come through winter in most districts and mature early next year, before the arrival of blackfly. Sow shallower than in spring, in a wide drill 1½in (4cm) deep. They can be cloched in January, but not before or plants will be weak.

When runner beans have finished don't store the plastic support nets without first untangling the old stems, which will harbour the eggs of many pests. If strings were used it is best to cut and burn them.

Keep hoeing between the rows of growing crops, particularly lettuces, spring cabbage, spring onions and Japanese onions. Hand-weed in the rows, as they have only a short period before winter in which to get established and cannot stand the competition of weeds.

Frost can lift onion seedlings out of the ground, so check and firm them back in.

Dig even small patches of ground as soon as they are cleared of crops or weeds, especially chickweed, will get a hold in mild weather. If you do have to leave any ground undug, hoe down weeds before they get going.

Looking after brussels sprouts
Keep brussels sprouts in good health by deterring pests and diseases and keeping pigeons at bay with netting. Plastic cups over the tops of stakes will make moving the netting easy. Many varieties, like Rampart, will be ready for harvesting now. Pick buttons from the base of the stem upwards as they develop.

1 **Tall plants in exposed, windy areas are best individually staked to prevent storm damage. As there is likely to be some whitefly infestation on this and other brassicas, regularly spray with an insecticide.**

2 **Remove leaves as they yellow and clear all litter that accumulates under the plants. If left, they will harbour pests and diseases.**

3 **As the harder weather sets in, pigeons will become a nuisance, especially in country districts. Give plants protection by netting, placing upturned plastic cups over the stakes for ease in moving the net.**

DECEMBER
Jobs for the month

There's relatively little work to do in the vegetable garden now, but keep checking vegetables in store and protect them from pests, diseases and hard weather. Outside, the less hardy crops may need some additional protection.

Cut down any remaining stems of globe artichokes and surround the crowns with a blanket of straw or bracken to give protection from deep, penetrating frosts.

Periodically check over vegetables in store. Mould on onion skins is a sign of a damp atmosphere, so move them to a drier place. Discard any bulbs that feel soft, or trouble will spread.

Straw down rows of trenched celery if not already done. The mulch will prevent the ground freezing deeply and help to prevent lifting.

Fruit

PLANTING TOP FRUIT

There should be room for top fruit in even a small garden if you stick to restricted forms such as cordon or bush apples, espalier pears or fan-trained morello cherries, plums and peaches. All of these, except the bush apples, can be grown on a wall or wires. Unfortunately culinary apples do not take to restrictive pruning like the dessert varieties.

Where space is not a problem, half- or full-standard trees can be planted to give high yields. Remember though, the larger the tree the more difficult it will be to prune, spray and pick.

Many varieties are self-infertile and need pollen from another variety flowering at the same time to ensure a good fruit set, so two or more different trees may be required. If you don't have room for two, choose a self-fertile variety.

When choosing top fruit, avoid early flowering ones if your ground is situated in a frost pocket or subject to late frosts. If the ground is poor ask for varieties grafted on to vigorous growing rootstocks. If the soil is particularly rich, go for those on a dwarfing stock to prevent excessive foliage growth which can result in poor cropping.

Apples can be planted at any time between November and March in a bare-rooted condition, but container-grown stock has the advantage of being plantable at almost any time, provided the ground is not waterlogged or frozen or you are not in the middle of a heatwave.

Pears need more nitrogen than apples, so grassing down or planting in lawns should be done only when restricted growth forms like dwarf pyramids are chosen.

Plums do not like acid soils, but this can be rectified by liming. The best flavour is obtained from fan-trained trees against a warm wall, but excellent results can be had from trees grown as half-standards, or bush forms. The more restricted tree forms are not suitable for plums and their relatives.

Unfortunately sweet cherries are not suitable for small gardens as all forms reach large trees that are hard to protect from birds and hard to pick. Large, fan-trained specimens are fine for extensive wall areas, but in a small space plant the smaller culinary morello cherries in a fan. These are self-fertile, so single trees are practicable.

Planting distances

With apples and pears the planting distance will depend on the tree form and rootstock, but the following recommendations are made for amateur gardeners: oblique cordons 2–3ft (60–90cm) apart in rows no closer than 6ft (1.8m); espaliers about 15ft (4.6m) apart; dwarf pyramids 3½–5ft (1–1.5m) apart in rows spaced 7–9ft (2.1–2.7m) from each other; dwarf bushes 10–12ft (3–3.6m) each way; bushes 12–18ft (3.6–5.5m) each way; and half-standards 30–40ft (9.2–12.2m) each way.

With plums and gages, space bush forms 12–18ft (3.6–5.5m) apart and half-standards at 18–24ft (5.5–7.3m). Allow 15ft (4.6m) between fan-trained

Cox's Orange Pippin apples

specimens. Fan-trained sweet cherries need 20–25ft (6.1–7.6m) spacing, while the free-standing bush or half-standard forms need 30–40ft (9.1–12.2m). Fan-trained morellos need at least 15ft (4.6m) and as bushes, 15–18ft (4.6–5.5m) spacing.

Recommended varieties

Apples Except in the two cases pointed out, the following dessert and culinary varieties have overlapping flowering periods and will therefore pollinate each other.
Dessert types Lord Lambourne—ready to eat by October–November; Cox's Orange Pippin—a high-quality apple, November–January eating; Crispin—a triploid needing two other pollinators, ready October–February; James Grieve—for September picking and hardy; Sunset—a similar flavour to Cox.
Culinary types Bramley's Seedling—probably one of the best-known cookers grown, but a triploid, ready November–March; Howgate Wonder—ready October–January; Blenheim Orange—triploid, ready November–January; Crawley Beauty—late-flowered, but self-fertile, ready December–March; Newton Wonder—needs a pollinator to crop well, ready November–March.

Pears If only one variety can be planted, then either Conference or William's Bon Chrétien are recommended, otherwise plant varieties that flower at the same time.
Early flowering Louise Bonne of Jersey—ready in October, plant with one of the following group for good results.
Mid-season Conference—ready October–November, not

A cluster of tasty damsons

Cherry Early Rivers (*Photo* Brian Furner)

Plum Cambridge Gage (*Photo* H Smith)

strictly self-fertile but able to set parthenogenically; Improved Fertility—a true self-fertile variety ready September–October; William's Bon Chrétien—ready September, good flavour.

Late Beurre Hardy—ready October, one of the hardiest; Doyenne du Comice—ready November, needs a pollinator.

Plums and gages *Dessert types* Denniston's Superb —self-fertile and prolific, mid-August; Early Transparent Gage—self-fertile, mid-August; Victoria—self-fertile, dual-purpose plum with heavy crops in August.

Culinary types Czar—self-fertile and hardy; Merryweather Damson—August–September, good for bottling or freezing; River's Early Prolific—late July–August.

Cherries The following sweet cherries will act as pollinators to each other: Bigarreau Napoleon—a regular cropper in July; Merton Bigarreau—mid-season (July) variety with almost black fruit; Merton Glory—large cream fruit splashed with crimson, crops in June.

Morello is an acid cherry that crops well August–September, the fruit being used for jam and fillings while the flowers will pollinate the three sweet cherry varieties given above.

Opposite

Tropaeolum speciosum (the flame flower) is a member of the nasturtium family and prefers a sheltered position.

Planting top fruit

1 Soak bare roots thoroughly and water containers before planting.

2 Check over the roots and remove damaged ones. Also reduce thick, downward growing ones on bare-rooted trees. Containerised stock should be checked for any perennial weeds.

3 Containerised root balls should be deep enough to bring the top of the compost level with the soil surface. Note the generous area of the planting hole.

Opposite

Above Mesembryanthemums, whether the brilliant Livingstone daisies of rockeries and borders or this succulent trailing form, are real eye-catchers with vivid, almost florescent colours.
Below Rightly described as the queen of all garden flowers is the graceful rose

4 Once the root ball or cluster is at the right depth, insert a suitable stake. Use stout wooden stakes with the trimmed ends generously treated with preservative.

5 Dwarf tree forms may require only one tie, but taller forms, like this half-standard, will need two. The upper one should be positioned just under the branch framework.

6 Use broad, strong ties that will not bite into the tree to cause chaffing. The latter problem can be solved by nailing the tie to the stake to reduce movement to a minimum. If the weather is dry at planting time, draw out a basin of soil round the tree and fill this with water. After sufficient water has been applied, replace the soil and mulch.

Planting and supporting trained trees

1 Trained trees like cordons and fans will need the support of wires tautly secured between posts set either side in concrete or driven 3ft (90cm) into the ground. Pre-trained container-ised specimens can be planted at almost any time. Bare-rooted trees are planted from leaf-fall until early spring.

2 Secure long canes to the wires where cordon or fan trees are required. Fans will need several canes radiating up and out from the main stem. Use eyed bolts to keep wires taut.

3 Tie the shoots securely into the canes, but take care not to do the job so well that the stems cannot expand without being constricted, or these weak spots are liable to snap later. Once the plant is firmly in position, loosen up the soil surface by forking over where you have walked.

PLANTING SOFT FRUIT

The black currant is probably the most popular of bush soft fruits and will tolerate some shade. Allow at least 5ft (1.5m) between plants and start with bushes certified free of virus. It is important to grow them as a stool, so make sure that the stems are buried with at least two or three buds underground. After planting, the stems are cut down to within 1–2in (2.5–5cm) of the ground.

Red and white currants need the same spacing, but here the plants are encouraged to produce a main stem (leg). Similarly, gooseberries should have a prominent leg. Both sorts of fruit should have the lateral shoots reduced by half their length at planting time. Occasionally special-ist suppliers offer single, double or even triple cordon gooseberries. If space is short, go for these trained forms, especially to go against a fence or low wall.

Recommended varieties

Black currants *Early* Boskoop Giant—only a moder-ate cropper.

Red Lake, a popular mid-season red currant with long trusses of fruit

Mid-season Wellington XXX vigorous with sweet, medium-to-large berries, a good cropper.
Late Baldwin—compact habit, needs rich soil.
Red currants Laxton's No 1—early, heavy cropping; Red Lake—mid-season type; Rondom—a recent intro-duction for late in the season.
White currants White varieties of the red currant. Try White Versailles—an early cropper—or White Dutch—mid-season variety.
Gooseberries Careless—large, smooth-skinned berries, early-to-mid-season; Keepsake—late to ripen but early for picking green for cooking, needs regular spray pro-gramme against American mildew; Leveller—dislikes poor, light soils, has large, almost smooth berries; Whin-ham's Industry—mid-season variety with hairy, sweet fruit.

Planting gooseberries

1 For preference, grow gooseberries on ground cultivated for a couple of years. Dig in humus material and firm down before planting two- or three-year-old bushes. Allow about 5ft (1.5m) between bushes in rows spaced 6ft (1.8m) apart. Cordons will require less room—single types only 12in (30cm) apart.

2 Take out a planting hole wide enough for the roots of lifted plants when spread out and deep enough to drop containerised bushes to the correct level. Fork in a little bonemeal plus some peat if the ground is a little on the light side.

3 Check over the plants and remove any dead or damaged portions with secateurs. Defoliaged, shrivelled shoot tips could indicate American mildew, so remove. Check containerised bushes for weeds and remove any suckers. Cut them off at the point where they spring from the main root system.

4 Gooseberries should be planted so that the nursery soil mark (bare rooted plants) is at or just above ground level. They should have a 'leg' or trunk for several inches to keep the branch framework well above the ground. This makes cultivation and picking easy. Firm down the infill soil by treading and water well in if the ground is dry.

Planting loganberries and blackberries

Provided you can supply the roots with a rich growing medium, some cane fruits can be grown in a restricted area. Loganberries and blackberries are ideal for those narrow beds that often occur between the garden path and boundary fence or wall. The fence will make an ideal support, but in the open garden a framework of posts and galvanised wire will be necessary.

Provide posts at 10ft (3m) intervals and secure wires at 3ft (90cm), 4ft (1.2m) and 5ft (1.5m) from the ground. Posts should be about 8ft (2.4m) long. Plant both fruits 10ft (3m) apart in the middle of each wire bay and prune back the shoots to 9in (23cm).

No need for scratched hands with this Oregon Thornless blackberry

Recommended varieties

Blackberries Bedford Giant—earliest variety, fruits July until late August, prickly, but with juicy berries; Himalayan Giant—strong and prickly, fruiting late July into October; Oregon Thornless—heavy fruit clusters as sweet as the wild bramble but without the vicious prickles.

Loganberries Thornless Loganberry—clone LY654 usually offered, which freely produces large red fruits.

Planting raspberries

Unlike many other fruit crops, raspberries will succeed in a partially shaded spot. Like blackberries, this crop needs a soil high in organic matter. Work the organic materials into the ground before planting, as the roots are near soil level and easily damaged by deep cultivations once established. Plant so that the roots are about 3in (7.5cm) beneath the ground and space out to about 18in (45cm) apart in rows 6ft (1.8m) distant.

Raspberries need spacing out at 18in (45cm) intervals, with the roots about 3in (7.5cm) deep. After planting, cut raspberry canes down to 6–12in (15–30cm) from the ground to promote new shoot growth

Summer-fruiting varieties like Glen Cova need a wire and post support, but this isn't necessary for autumn croppers

Recommended varieties

Mid-season Malling Jewel—heavy cropper, good for freezing; Malling Promise—early, large, firm berries; Glen Clova—long cropping season and suitable for freezing, jams and bottling; Malling Orion—resistant to several virus-carrying aphids and mildew, good for freezing and bottling, but not for jam; Malling Admiral—another newcomer, which crops late in the season.

Autumn fruiting September—crops from September through to first frosts; Zeva—a vigorous Swiss variety, which may crop from July until November.

A strawberry barrel is ideal if space is at a premium. Plant the runners as you gradually fill the barrel with compost

Planting strawberries

Even if you have no garden it is possible to grow a good crop of strawberries. They are easily accommodated in a wooden barrel with 1in (2.5cm) holes drilled through the sides at intervals, proprietary plastic tubs with special planting holes or other suitable containers.

When planting a barrel, put in a central cylinder of wire netting and fill this to within 6in (15cm) of the top with coarse gravel or broken rubble to ensure good drainage. Put a layer of drainage material at the bottom and gradually add compost, planting a young runner at each station as you work your way up the barrel. Finish off with three or four plants at the top and never allow the compost to dry out.

If you're planting strawberries the conventional way, make sure the site is well drained and supplied with humus-forming materials. If more than one row is needed, space them out 30in (75cm) apart and allow 18–24in (45–60cm) between plants.

Plant so that the crown of the runner is at soil level and if they are 'bare-rooted', spread the roots evenly over a low ridge of soil running across the planting hole.

Strawberries planted in spring should not be allowed to set fruit, except for the autumn bearing varieties like Gento and Rabunda.

Recommended varieties

Summer fruiting Royal Sovereign—an old variety with excellent flavour, but prone to disease; Cambridge Vigour—early initially, but mid-season after first year; Grandee—enormous fruits, particularly in second year; Cambridge Favourite—probably the heaviest cropper but not particularly good flavour; Tamella—can produce an additional crop in autumn.

Perpetual fruiting Gento—needs more attention to feeding and watering than the summer varieties.

Alpine types These small fruits are delicious from June onwards. Baron Solemacher (non-running), Delicious and Alexandria—all can be raised from seed to fruit the following year.

JANUARY

Jobs for the month

Pruning of top and stone fruit can continue, but if fruit is diseased, leave it until summer.

Tip raspberry canes and renew ties if necessary.

Finish pruning gooseberries and red currants.

Forcing rhubarb

By forcing established crowns into growth you can have a succession of blanched rhubarb sticks early in the year. Where plants are lifted and forced under cover, allow the crowns to make a little growth in frost-free conditions before raising the temperature to 55–60°F (13–16°C).

1 If you don't have forcing facilities, rhubarb can be encouraged into early growth by mulching with rotted manure, then covering with a bin surrounded by straw.

2 If heat is available, lift strong three-year-old crowns and expose them to the cold for a couple of days.

A winter tar oil wash can be sprayed on top and soft fruit.

If peaches, nectarines and almonds show signs of bursting at the end of the month, spray against leaf curl with a copper or sulphur fungicide.

Grape vines can be propagated now by cutting a healthy, well-ripened shoot into 2–3in (5–7.5cm) sections, each of which needs a firm, healthy bud, termed an eye. Eye cuttings started now in a propagator at about 60°F (16°C) will give plants ready for planting in spring.

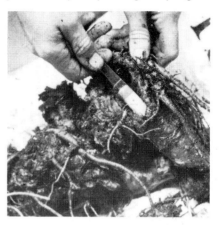

3 Carefully cut away all damaged or diseased roots—discard plants with hollow roots as this is a sign of crown rot disease.

4 Box up the crowns with the rounded bud just showing above the good compost mix and either place in a black polythene bag or under greenhouse staging 'blacked out' with sacking to exclude light. Keep the soil moist and first pickings will be in about a month. The sticks are ready when the leaves begin to turn dark.

FEBRUARY

Jobs for the month

Gooseberries not inside a fruit cage will need protecting from birds as the buds begin to swell. Bushes can be covered temporarily with netting, or black thread can be stretched tight between the branches. Bird repellant sprays help to some extent.

If not already done, get planting finished as soon as the weather permits.

Prune autumn-fruiting raspberries, cutting canes down almost to the ground.

Starting early strawberries

Early strawberries are the first fruit in the year to need attention, for they will start into growth in most areas in February, particularly if the weather is mild. As soon as the ground is dry enough, get to work on the rows planted especially for early fruiting. Pull away all dead leaves and any weeds.

Apply sulphate of potash at 1oz per sq yd (30gm per sq m). Alternatively, apply a fertiliser with a high potash content. Work this into the surface soil with a hoe and in doing so, draw the soil to the crown of the plants.

Don't cover the plants too soon with cloches or tunnels, or put the light on the frame, at this stage. A spell of mild weather with above average sunshine will induce rapid growth, which will be severely checked or even destroyed by short periods of cold later. In the south, mid to late February is the best time to cover, but in the Midlands and the north, late February to early March will be in time.

If your soil is open and light, water it thoroughly first. It is a good idea to spread straw and garden compost alongside the rows to conserve moisture and save the soil from excessive consolidation, as well as reduce weeds.

As the weather improves and day temperatures rise, ventilation will be necessary. With cloches the gaps between them are usually sufficient until flowering time, but with tunnels the sides need to be raised a little to allow air movement. Flowering time calls for general ventilation to allow the free movement of pollinating insects to ensure a good set of fruit.

Grey mould disease (botrytis) can prove troublesome under tunnels and cloches. Prevention is the best, so spray the plants thoroughly with a fungicide just before the flowers open, and again ten days later.

1 Check that strawberries supplied by post are in perfect condition.

2 Set them in a sunny position in well-manured soil, spacing the plants 12–18in (30–45cm) apart, with a minimum of 2ft (60cm) between the rows. Use a measured and marked plank to help with the spacing.

3 Plant firmly with the crown just at soil level.

4 Established strawberries—those planted last September or before—can be cloched in February to give an earlier crop.

MARCH
Jobs for the month
Production of new raspberry growth as well as fruiting potential can be reduced by cane spot, a fungus disease. If present, spray with lime sulphur or captan as the canes begin to shoot.

If cold weather is preventing insects from pollinating apricots, peaches and nectarines growing up walls, which will flower this month, hand-pollinate them.

Tar oil sprays can still be used on apple and pear trees if you forgot to apply a winter wash earlier.
Feeding fruit
All fruit trees and bushes need an adequate supply of nutrients. The ones that suffer the most from a low level of fertility are the soft fruits.

The best time to do this is from mid-February to mid-March. The main requirements are nitrogen, phosphorous, potash and magnesium. Other minor elements are best applied through a general fertiliser in which they are incorporated.

Apples The chief need of dessert apples in cultivated soil is potash. This should be applied at 1oz per sq yd (30gm per sq m) and worked into the soil. Nitrogen needs to be used with care. Nitro-chalk or sulphate of ammonia at 1½oz per sq yd (45gm per sq m) is usually sufficient, although less will be required on heavy soils. If the trees are growing in grass, less potash will be needed, while the nitrogen may have to be applied at from 2–4oz per sq yd (60–120gm per sq m) depending on the size of the tree. Cooking apples should have more nitrogen, both on cultivated soils and in grass.

Pears Pears need slightly more nitrogen than apples and, on most soils, less potash. During the first few years after planting, an annual dressing of superphosphate at 1oz per sq yd (30gm per sq m) helps to get the trees established. Magnesium deficiency occurs on some of the lighter soils and this can be rectified by applying magnesium limestone at 8oz per sq yd (230gm per sq m).

Potash may be required from time to time and a dressing of sulphate of potash at 1–1½oz per sq yd (30–45gm per sq m) every third year will meet this need.

Other top fruit This group, which includes plums, gages, damsons, apricots, peaches and nectarines, needs adequate supplies of nitrogen. A dressing of sulphate of ammonia or nitro-chalk at 1–2oz per sq yd (30–60gm per sq m) is needed each year if the trees are carrying heavy crops. Lime is also essential and, although over-liming should be avoided, a dressing of ground limestone or magnesium limestone should be given every third year at 8oz to the sq yd (227gm per sq m)

On lighter soils some plum cultivars suffer from potash deficiency, which can be identified by the typical marginal scorching of leaves from mid-summer onwards. This can be rectified by applying sulphate of potash at 1–2oz per sq yd (30–60gm per sq m) in early February each year until the trouble is cured.

Peaches and nectarines benefit from applications of superphosphate at 1–2oz per sq yd (30–60gm per sq m) for the first few years after planting.

It's a good idea to feed top fruit at this time of the year to ensure heavy cropping later on—as on this Doyenne du Comice pear

Black currants Soft fruits have similar requirements to top fruit. They are, in general, gross feeders, and so need dressings of fertilisers and mulches of bulky organics if crops of high quality fruits are to be produced each year.

It is almost impossible to over-feed black currants. The chief need is nitrogen to produce plenty of young wood each year. A spring dressing of nitro-chalk on the heavy soils or sulphate of ammonia on the lighter ones at 1–2oz per sq yd (30–60gm per sq m) will meet early needs. A further 1oz per sq yd (30gm per sq m) can be applied after the crop has been picked.

Red currants and gooseberries These can be grouped together for nutritional needs. Potash is important and they quickly show marginal scorching if there is a deficiency. Nitrogen is also needed to ensure that sufficient young wood is produced and fruit quality maintained. The balance between potash and nitrogen is also important and an application of 1oz (30gm) of sulphate of potash and 1–2oz (30–60gm) of sulphate of ammonia each spring is needed.

Raspberries These delicious soft fruits often show signs of starvation—poor cane growth and small, rather dried up fruit. An application of fertiliser, as for the gooseberries, in spring plus a further dressing of nitrogen after the crop has been picked, will assist cane production for the next year.

Finish pruning soft fruits

You should finish pruning soft fruits like black currants this month if you didn't do it last August after fruiting. Watch out for signs of big bud, and make preventative sprays when growth starts and again when flower buds show to deter mites.

1 If not done in early autumn prune black currants now to let in light and air. Remove all unproductive wood and shorten some branches back to recently formed laterals to give good shape.

2 Look out for big bud, a condition caused by mites and often leading to reversion virus, which reduces cropping. Where only small amounts of big bud appear, rub out the affected buds by hand; prune out shoots heavily infested. To prevent big bud mites, spray bushes with lime sulphur now.

3 To promote strong, healthy growth, give bushes an application of nitro-chalk at the rate of 1oz per sq yd (30gm per sq m). Black currants are best when heavily manured; well decomposed farmyard manure is best and should be applied as a mulch when available.

APRIL
Jobs for the month

Small trees, bushes and trees on walls should, if possible, be protected from frost with muslin or something similar. Cover the young blossom.

Dryness at the roots is fatal to newly planted trees. They need at least 4 gal (18.2 l) each over the root area and perhaps more later on. A thick mulch of manure or compost will help.

Check all tree ties that may have worked loose through the winter, or may be too tight, and retread root area where rocking and loosening may have occurred.

Gooseberries must have potash to do well. 2oz (57gm) of sulphate of potash to each bush will keep them happy through the year.

Spray apples at pink bud stage and pears at white bud stage with lime sulphur to control scab.

Strawberries under cloches may need a thorough watering to swell fruit. Watch also for greenfly swarming under the leaves and spray accordingly. Newly planted strawberries must have first flowers taken off to allow plants to become established.

MAY
Jobs for the month
Melon seeds sown in the middle of the month in a pot on a windowsill will give plants ready just in time for planting in cold frames or under cloches early in June. Varieties for this cold culture method are best chosen from the cantaloupe range—Golden Crispy, Sweetheart and Ha-Ogen, for example.

If strawberry plants were planted earlier in the spring, remove flowers to allow energy to go into producing vigorous growth. Perpetual varieties can be fruited in late summer.

Where small apricot fruits are clustered closely together they will need thinning. A few can be taken off now, but the final thinning should not take place until the stones have formed next month.

Bark ringing of apple trees can be done in May. It is necessary when trees are growing strongly and producing few flowers, with, consequently, a poor crop. Take out a ring of bark, no more than $\frac{1}{2}$in (13mm) wide and down as far as the wood, from the main stem and seal the cut with adhesive tape. A single branch that is growing more strongly than the others can be ringed in the same way.

Spring disbudding of peaches and nectarines
The growth of wood buds will start on peaches and nectarines as soon as flowering is over. They grow quickly and to prevent trained, wall-grown trees expending energy on producing unwanted wood you should start to disbud them early over a period of three weeks to a month.

Shoots should be 1–1$\frac{1}{2}$in (2.5–4cm) long, just large enough to get hold of with the thumb and forefinger. They are easily removed with a slight twist. The best way is to go over each branch, individually removing any young shoots growing inwards towards the wall and all those growing outwards. A week or so later, go over the trees again.

You want the tree to develop only sufficient shoots to replace the current fruiting wood plus any extra branches you may wish to add to the existing framework. This means keeping the leading shoot on each fruiting branch and perhaps one or two at the base of the shoot.

Apricots, cherries and plums benefit from the same treatment, for the removal of unwanted shoots at this juvenile time reduces the need for hard pruning during the dormant season.

Keep on top of pests and diseases
Spraying against pests and diseases should be a regular job. Mildews are particularly common and best prevented, but if they do occur, take immediate steps to control them with a systemic fungicide.

1 Spray apples with a combined insecticide/fungicide to prevent mildew and capsids. Apply at pink bud or petal fall stages. Remove any shoots that are affected with mildew and burn them.

2 Dust strawberries with flowers of sulphur or dinocap at bud stage or just after flowering to control mildew. Symptoms include dark upper surfaces (grey below) and curled leaves.

3 Dust gooseberries with sulphur or spray with lime sulphur to prevent American blight (mildew). On sulphur-shy varieties like Leveller and Careless, use dinocap or washing soda.

JUNE
Jobs for the month
Spray raspberries with derris ten days after flowering starts, to combat raspberry maggot.

Apple mildew—spray now to prevent it (*Photo* Brian Furner)

Continue spraying apples and pears against mildew and scab, and also against apple codling moth caterpillars in mid-month, repeating two or three weeks later.

Strawberry runners should be removed and the plants netted against birds. The runners can be used to produce new plants.

Don't be alarmed by the 'June drop'
New fruit growers may well be alarmed by the fact that between early June and early July most of their trees appear to be shedding their fruits. No need to worry unduly because this 'June drop' as it is called is nature's way of thinning out crops to the numbers that the trees can support. In fact you often have to carry out even more thinning where overcrowding is still evident.

The drop is particularly noticeable in apples and occurs in two stages. The first comes two or three weeks after petal-fall, when lots of small, pea-sized apples are seen below the tree. This is due to incomplete fertilisation. The main drop, however, comes in late June or early July, often in two distinct phases about ten days apart.

Plums and pears also drop fruitlets. A loss by pears between mid-May and the end of June should always be treated with concern, for it may be due to pear midge. The infested fruitlets become deformed and enlarged and will eventually fall. Cutting open will reveal a black cavity containing several maggots.

The adult midge can be controlled by spraying, at the white bud stage, with an insecticide such as malathion or rogor. Later, thorough cultivation of the soil area below the tree to a depth of 3in (7.5cm) will destroy the hibernating maggots. Treating with a soil insecticide during July is an alternative to cultivation.

JULY
Jobs for the month
Complete thinning of outdoor grape vines started last month, allowing no more than one bunch to each side shoot. Spray the vines with Bordeaux mixture against mildew and other fungal disorders.

Cover morello cherries with nets to protect the ripening fruits from birds.

Cut out and burn immediately any plum branches suffering from silver leaf disease. Symptoms are a metallic silvering of the foliage.

Once dessert cherries have finished fruiting, spray with derris or malathion against blackfly.

The easiest method of strawberry propagation is from the runners that appear at this time of year. New plants appear on the runners and all you have to do is to let them root and then separate them from the parent.

Summer pruning
Of all the jobs performed by the conscientious fruit-grower, summer pruning is possibly the most important. It is not just a case of cutting back the season's long shoots; this is the time to ensure that the training is done properly. Shoots for building up the framework can be selected and surplus shoots removed. Spurs that have failed to grow and shoots that have died back during spring can also be taken off.

Young shoots of cordon gooseberries are often vulnerable to strong winds, so any broken ones should be tidied up and shoots left in the best places to form replacement spurs. All other shoots not needed for extension of the basic framework should be cut back to six leaves. Overcrowded shoots should be thinned out. Red and white currants can be treated similarly.

Apricot laterals need to be reduced to four to six leaves and the wounds treated. It pays to go over the trees at least twice during the season because winter pruning on any scale is not to be recommended.

The disbudding carried out on peaches early in the season should have taken care of any badly-placed shoots. Take a look though, to see if any good new growth at the back is worth training to the front. Free-standing and wall-trained young plums on dwarfing stock need summer pruning to keep the trees compact and to encourage fruit spurs.

Outdoor vines also need a continual summer pruning process to keep growth within bounds and divert nutrients to the developing berries.

Now to those important top fruits, apples and pears. By reducing the annual growth at this time of year, when the tree is in full leaf, its growth rate and vigour can be controlled before it gets out of hand. Summer pruning also encourages the formation of next year's fruit buds.

Being planted close together, cordon trees must always be summer pruned, as must bushes and half-standards. As pears develop fruit buds more readily, bush tree pruning can be modified to allow the shape to build up.

Pruning and general maintenance of apples

Now that new growth is well developed on apples, prune back lateral shoots to encourage flowering next year; on large trees prune back to about 5in (12.5cm). Continue pest and disease control, de-suckering and watering as necessary.

1 Apples, when trained in a restricted form like cordons, will need some summer pruning. Reduce lateral shoots back to the third leaf, ignoring the cluster of leaves at the base.

2 Don't prune the leading shoots on restricted forms, especially in young trees, as they give the extension growth for height.

3 Although the 'June drop' will thin out fruitlets naturally, you may still need to reduce the numbers.

4 Remove suckers that appear at the base of trees as close to the rootstock as possible. Soak the roots of small trees with water in dry periods.

5 It's important that fruit trees do not suffer from a lack of water so, to improve fruit yields, soak the roots thoroughly in dry periods. Pay special attention to newly planted trees.

6 Give preventative sprays of fenitrothion or malathion to discourage codling moth grubs in fruitlets; BHC, malathion or dimethoate will control both codling moth and red spider.

AUGUST

Jobs for the month

If woolly aphis (American blight) is seen on apple trees, pressure spray with malathion or scrub small patches with a wire brush dipped in methylated spirits.

Cut old fruited raspberry canes down to ground level and thin out the weakest of the new shoots.

Once strawberries have finished fruiting, cut off the foliage, feed and water to start strong new growth. Some varieties will crop again under the protection of cloches in the autumn.

When to pick apples

Picking apples at the right time is crucial. If they are gathered too early or left on the tree too long, the eating quality is poor. Late August or early September, according to area, brings the first ripe crops. As a general rule these early maturing varieties do not keep for long, and as the fruit on any one tree is seldom ready at the same time, several pickings must be made. The front-runners include Beauty of Bath, George Cave, Laxton's Advance and Discovery.

During the later part of September and early October, cultivars such as Early Worcester, Merton Worcester, Worcester Pearmain, James Grieve, Egremont Russet and Ellison's Orange will be ready, as will culinary apples like Arthur Turner, Lord Derby and Rev. Wilks. Later still, extending the season to beyond Christmas, are Cox's Orange Pippin, Laxton's Superb and Winston, with culinary varieties Bramley Seedling, Crawley Beauty and Monarch.

The first signs of fruit ripening will often be the increased activity of birds around the tree. A change in colour is also an indication. A test should be made by lifting individual fruits and giving a slight twist. Those that are ready will come away easily without any pulling being necessary.

Pruning and taking cuttings of black currants

Black currant bushes should be pruned as soon as possible after the fruit has been picked. The aim is to encourage the bushes to produce good strong shoots from below soil level, or as near to soil level as possible. This production of young shoots is required every year, for the best fruit always grows on new wood.

1 If not done already, prune established bushes. Remove old spent shoots and thin out overcrowded growth made this year to keep the bush tidy.

2 Cuttings of the healthiest new shoots can be taken now. Reduce shoots to about 8in (20cm) by cutting just under a bud, then remove all but the top few leaves.

3 Make a 6in (15cm) deep cleft in the garden and add some sharp sand if the ground is on the heavy side. Choose a well-drained site, sheltered if possible.

4 Place the cuttings at 12in (30cm) intervals in the cleft, leaving 2–3in (5–7.5cm) of the tops showing above ground level. Firm in the soil to prevent the cuttings drying out.

SEPTEMBER
Jobs for the month
Strawberry runners that you have rooted yourself or bought in can be planted now or any time in autumn while soil conditions are favourable. Give them as much organic material as possible.

Plant strawberry runners so that the crown is not buried, and firm in by hand

Continue to pick apples and pears. Pears for storing should be gathered just as the skins begin to turn yellow around the stalk but while the main part of the fruit is still green. They should then be placed in a cool, dark room in single layers.

Seedlings—a fruitless exercise?
All fruit trees and bushes produce seedling plants from their pips, seeds or stones, often naturally through the activities of birds, and sometimes by gardeners sowing to increase their stock. Is it worth the amateur's time, space and effort of growing then on, however?

The seedlings will all make strong plants, which will probably fruit eventually, but almost without exception the fruit will be inferior to that of the parent plant from which the seed came. If soft fruit is grown, there are always plenty of gooseberry and black or red currant seedlings springing up. Growing any of these on is almost certain to be a waste of time and space. Treat them as weeds and dispatch them.

No fruit seeds produce true to variety. The chances that the seedling will be better than the parent are about a million to one.

Of course all fruit varieties were originally seedlings, but professional growers have more know-how, space and patience to take a chance that that very long shot will come up.

The popular culinary apple Bramley Seedling—a million to one long shot that came up (*Photo* H Smith)

117

OCTOBER
Jobs for the month
Cut off the old fruited canes of blackberries and logan-berries and tie the new ones in their places.

Picking and storing top fruit
Picking and storing are two important jobs in the fruit garden at present. It is essential to store only unblemished fruit, otherwise you could lose the lot through rot. Cool, airy conditions are needed.

Give peaches a spray of Bordeaux mixture or lime-sulphur just as the leaves start to fall as a final protection against leaf curl.

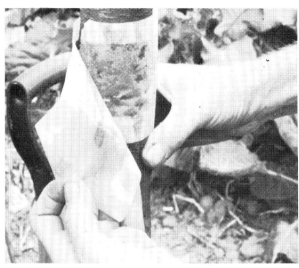

1   Winter moth caterpillars can cause havoc to fruit such as apples, so greaseband your trees now to prevent the wingless female moths climbing the trunk and laying eggs.

3   Periodically check over fruit in store, especially pears, which are best laid out unwrapped in trays so they're not touching. Store indoors in a cool, dry place.

2   Keep fruit trees free of weeds by applying a weedkiller around the base, but always check directions on packet. For general weed control use products based on aminotriazole and sima-zine; use dalapon on grasses like couch.

4   Many apple varieties will be ready for picking now. Test for ripeness by lifting and slightly twisting the fruit. The stalk should part easily from the tree. Store wrapped in newspaper or special oiled wraps.

118

NOVEMBER

Jobs for the month

There is time now to take stock of permanent structures such as the support for training wires. Check all posts to see that they have not rotted at ground level. Where reinforcement is needed, drive in a shorter post or angle iron next to the faulty one and securely bolt the two together.

The ground can be prepared for planting all types of trees, bushes and canes. Dig it deeply and work in manure and other humus materials.

Keeping fruit trees clean also means clearing up fallen leaves from under them. Dead leaves and other debris provide ideal over-wintering quarters for many pests. A light digging round each tree will remove another refuge—weeds.

Pruning young apples

Providing leaf drop is well under way, you can begin to prune young or isolated apple trees showing an overcrowded branch system. Take out all dead or diseased wood and open up the centre. Delay pruning old trees, or those in groups until next month or later to lessen the risk of canker infection.

1 Take a long look at the tree before starting. Make a note of those branches that can be removed to open up the head but still leave a good shape.

2 Start by removing the larger branches, especially those that are crossing or filling the centre of the framework. Make an undercut with the pruning saw to avoid tearing bark.

3 Make the second cut from the top of the branch to complete the job. Note that the branch is removed as close to the main stem as possible to avoid a snag.

4 Trim the bark surrounding the wound with a sharp knife to remove any rough edges that could 'catch' disease spores that are floating in the air. Use secateurs to prune out any smaller branches and shoots that are overcrowded. Suckers growing out of the rootstock should be cut away at their junction with the roots.

119

DECEMBER
Jobs for the month

Make regular checks on fruit in store and remove any showing signs of deterioration.

Outdoor vines can be pruned. Cut back all the year's new growth to two eyes and take out all weak and spindly wood.

Most trees will benefit from a sprinkling of sulphate of potash over the root area.

Birds seeking winter food may begin pecking out the newly emerging buds, particularly of gooseberries and plums. Cover bushes with netting and a bird repellant spray may be necessary for trees.

Check that grease bands are still properly positioned and free of fallen leaves.

Winter sprays

Spraying fruit trees and bushes with tar oil washes at this time of year is important especially if they have been neglected. Use a spray such as Mortegg at eight per cent strength for a couple of years, then reduce to five per cent, which is the right strength for normal use. Many people tar oil wash every winter, but once fruit trees are reasonably clean, every third year should be enough, relying on spring sprays for the other two years.

Tar oil sprays can be used on the top fruits—apples, pears, plums, cherries—and also the bush and some cane fruits. Some insect pests will be killed, but it is most effective against over-wintering eggs. Pests controlled are aphids, apple and pear sucker, winter moths and plum fruit moth. Other troublesome pests such as capsid, apple blossom weevil, apple sawfly and codling moth are not controlled and have to be dealt with in spring and summer.

Start spraying at the top and over each branch thoroughly, finishing up at the base of the trunk. To get good coverage you must move around the tree. You will need to wear old clothes and an eye shield. Choose a dry day, free from frost and with little or no wind. Crops growing beneath the trees should be protected with a polythene sheet. Winter washes can be either tar oil or DNC/Petroleum. The latter will control a slightly wider range of pests that overwinter on the trees, including red spider mite. These sprays should alway be applied while trees and bushes are dormant and December is the best month.

Prune and check trees

Provided the branches are not frosted, carry out the pruning of top fruit trees. Treat major wounds with waterproof tree paint to avoid infection. Remove all dead or diseased wood and spray to protect trees from an early pest invasion. All remaining windfall fruit should also be collected.

1 Newly planted top fruit in a restricted growth form may need some light pruning to maintain shape. Here, the sideshoots of an oblique cordon apple are reduced to form fruiting spurs, but the topmost one is left to make extension growth.

2 Where fruiting has been poor, root pruning half the tree may encourage productivity. Take out a trench and remove the larger roots carefully. Then fill in and tread the soil firm.

3 Spray the trees with a winter wash to kill off overwintering insect pests and control the unsightly green algae sometimes seen on the trunks. Check all ties and replace rotten ones with strong rubber or plastic ties.

Trees and shrubs

CHOOSING TREES AND SHRUBS

Before buying from the vast array to be seen in garden centres these days it pays to think carefully what you want from the plants. In many cases catalogues give lists of trees and shrubs that are ideal for specific uses, but you should also take into account whether those you like have any particular soil requirements.

Arbutus unedo **(strawberry tree) will tolerate a limy soil**

In the main, apart from a few ericas and the strawberry tree (arbutus), the ericaceous plants, the heathers, camellias, azaleas, rhododendrons, tend to dislike soils on the alkaline (limy) side, so you would avoid camellias and rhododendrons in, for instance, a garden on a chalky hillside.

The aspect of the site may also determine what you can plant, as many plants will not grow well or flower in dense shade. Conversely, many woodland shrubs may scorch badly in hot sun and shrivel up in front of your eyes. The choice for almost any soil, aspect or particular use is still, however, very large.

Small shrubs for small gardens

In the smaller garden go for those with a restricted growth habit. Lilacs are one of the more popular shrubs for May display, but in a small area try the dwarf-growing *Syringa velutina (S. palibiniana)* at 4–5ft (1.2–1.5m) or the more open *S. microphylla,* which flowers in June and again in late summer or early autumn.

Hebes (veronicas)—sun-lovers for small gardens (*Photo* H Smith)

In sunny, well-drained soil the compact, low-growing *Genista lydia* makes a mound of yellow flowers up to 2ft (60cm) high during May and June, a good companion for the sun rose, *Cistus corbariensis,* which, at almost twice the height, produces a profusion of red buds that open pure white. Another race of sun-lovers are the hebes (veronicas), which include the evergrey ground-cover variety Pagei.

Blue is a less common colour in the shrub world, but for sheer flower power, nothing quite meets the standards of the Californian lilac, ceanothus. *C. prostratus* is a creeping species for the smaller garden, but where more space is available, try the beautiful billowing hybrid, Delight. *Ceratostigma willmottianum* is another low-growing shrub with rich blue blooms.

Where you can provide a lime-free rooting run, then the heathers and ericas will provide almost year-round flowering and foliage colour. A collection of small rhododendrons or azaleas is also an ideal choice for an acid or neutral soil with *Rhododendron yakushimanum* proving itself a wonderful low-growing plant covered with rose-coloured buds that open into large white flowers in May.

If you want a fairly maintenance-free area, then ground-cover planting is best. The varied selection of periwinkles (vincas) are recommended in almost any situation or soil, as they soon form carpets of green or variegated evergreen foliage, studded with blooms in white, blue or purple. In sunny, dry spots, particularly on awkward sloping sites, try the rock roses, helianthemums, or spreading evergreen mats of our own native rock avens, *Dryas octopetala,* which covers itself with large, white, daisy flowers, closely followed by the silky seed-heads.

The easy, perhaps over-vigorous, Rose of Sharon, *Hypericum calycinum,* is another good cover plant for

Cotoneaster horizontalis **for covering unsightly objects** (*Photo* H Smith)

Pyracantha rogersiana **used as a hedge**

both sun and shade. For covering unsightly objects at ground level, try the Herringbone cotoneaster, *Cotoneaster horizontalis,* which also produces a crop of red berries in autumn, or the dense needle mats of *Juniperus communis depressa* or *J. horizontalis,* particularly the variety Bar Harbour.

Subjects for foliage and fruit

By choosing tree and shrubs with coloured foliage you get a long display season. The varieties of *Cornus alba* like elegantissima and aurea are plants that are desirable for their winter bark effect and also liven up a dull patch in summer with coloured foliage. Of the trees, the yellow leaves of the false acacia *Robinia frisia* are particularly outstanding (though it is brittle in windy spots), especially if planted with the purple-leaved smoke bush, *Cotinus coggygria* Royal Purple.

We should not forget the berried subjects. The choice here is wide, but some of the best types are the Mountain Ashes, like sorbus Joseph Rock with yellow clusters of fruits borne among autumn foliage tints of red, orange and purple, or the flowering crab apples, like malus John Downie, which has large, conical orange-red edible fruits. For the smaller garden the low-growing evergreen *Virbur-*

num davidii is unusual for its lovely blue clusters of berries, while the taller *V. betulifolium* produces masses of red currant-like clusters as the foliage drops. The numerous forms of cotoneaster and pyracantha will follow the massed flower clusters with heavy crops of yellow or red berries.

Trees as specimens

Even in the small garden there is a range of small trees to relieve the broad flat outlook of a lawn. Weeping trees are particularly suitable for such positions or, if you prefer something of a more upright nature, the fastigiate or 'flagpole' forms are an ideal choice.

For large areas the tall, sweeping species of conifer or larger magnolias come into their own, but such trees take many years to reach their ultimate height. Avoid putting these specimen plants right in the centre of the lawn, but rather put them towards the back and to one side for a more pleasing outlook from the house.

The weeping cherries are a good choice for a small garden, and Alford's Weeping form of Laburnum waterei or almost any of the laburnums make superb specimen trees. Back to the larger garden, the evergreen *Cedrus deodara pendula* makes a dramatic focal point to admire throughout the year. The upright-growing trees, too, are desirable, especially in restricted spaces or where you don't want to block out too much of the background plantings. The Flagpole Cherry, *Prunus amanogawa,* is one of the favourite choices.

For something unusual you might like to plant one of the so-called fossil trees like *Ginkgo biloba fastigiata,* with distinctive maidenhair-like foliage that takes on pleasant autumn tints before dropping. For attractive flowering trees, the magnolias are prime contenders, unless your soil is limy. In areas that suffer from late frosts, try the later-flowering species like *Magnolia wilsoni,* with white, saucer-shaped blooms and prominent crimson centres.

Cedrus deodara **makes an attractive focal point**

JANUARY
Jobs for the month

Snow may need shaking from branches before they break.

Walk round occasionally to check supporting stakes and ties.

Continue to prune bush and standard roses started in late autumn.

Shrubs such as roses, hydrangeas, lilacs, viburnums and Indian azaleas growing in pots can be moved into the greenhouse to induce earlier flowering.

Containerised climbing shrubs to camouflage a bleak wall or fence can be planted so long as the ground is not frozen. Provide support in the form of a trellis or wire framework and use evergreens such as variegated ivy if you want year-round coverage. The addition of peat, leaf-mould or compost will improve the soil.

At this time of the year we can expect strong, cold winds to cause severe damage to newly planted and tender shrubs. A screen of netting or hessian can reduce the wind force and prevent excessive drying out of foliage. Bracken or straw wrapped round the plant before the screen is secured will give additional protection in cold areas.

Tidy ericaceous shrubs

Ericaceous shrubs can be tidied up before growth restarts later in spring. Although not heavy feeders, the application of bonemeal and a mulch of peat will encourage more vigorous growth and better flowering.

1 Remove dead flower heads on heathers and ericas to keep the plants tidy and encourage shapely, bushy growth later in spring. Also remove any dead or straggling branches.

2 Apply a dressing of bonemeal to plants such as rhododendrons, heathers, and camellias and work it gently into the soil surface.

3 Also apply garden compost, peat or lime-free leafmould around these plants as a light mulch. Do not put these materials on frozen or frosted ground.

4 Ericaceous plants, like this camellia, may show pale leaves caused by the presence of lime in the soil (chlorosis). Water the soil with Iron Sequestrene to enable the plant to regain its dark green colour.

Layering clematis

This is a good time to propagate deciduous climbing shrubs like clematis by layering. By pegging down strong shoots into the ground or pots, good young plants will be ready for severing from the parent in about six months' time.

1 Select the healthiest looking shoots that can easily be pegged down to the ground without breaking the stems. Remove any dead leaves and stalks around the leaf joints.

2 Where layers are to be rooted direct into the ground, mix sharp sand and peat into the soil around the climber, where they are to be rooted.

3 Use a piece of galvanised wire or a hairpin to peg down the shoot, making sure that the leaf joint is buried. Partially cutting through the stem under the bud may speed rooting.

4 Tie the exposed portion of the shoot to a vertical support to stop wind and rain working the stem out of the soil before rooting occurs. Don't let the mound of soil dry out. To make transplanting easier later on, shoots can also be pegged down into pots of compost placed round the climber. Peg down securely at a convenient leaf joint.

5 By pegging down several leaf joints along a shoot (serpentine layering) you can build up a good stock of plants.

FEBRUARY
Jobs for the month

Shrubs blooming now that provide welcome cut flowers for indoors include forsythia, Bridal Wreath *(Spiraea arguta)* and Mexican Orange Blossom *(Choisya ternata)*.

Planting trees and shrubs

Planning The right choice of plant will determine from the start whether your shrubs will succeed. First look at what plants are recommended for your particular soil type. Much can be done, however, to improve soil conditions for a particular plant.

Make sure that they will not outgrow their alloted area by checking the ultimate height and spread. Some climbers are guilty of this, particularly the Russian vine *(Polygonum baldschuanicum)*.

Shrubs that produce a shallow mat of roots, like rhododendrons, are often lifted from the open ground. Make sure these have a compact root ball that will not dry out or break up before planting. Tall specimens with little in the way of fibrous roots will need substantial support for some time. Some plants naturally produce a sparse root system; brooms, gorse, cistus, spartium and tamarix are typical. They are best bought as young potted plants.

Correct siting is also important, especially in the early days when plants are less resistant to weather conditions. If your garden is exposed, some form of screening may be necessary for a season or two. Avoid siting early-flowering shrubs in a known frost pocket or in the path of prevailing cold winds, or blossom will be scorched in most years.

Preparing the soil Prepare the soil well in advance if possible. Dig the site thoroughly as early in the winter as you can. Where the ground is free-draining and light, such as sand, digging is best left until late winter or early spring.

Good drainage is vital, so on heavy soils the addition of organic materials like leafmould, peat, compost or old manure will help. Conditions are the reverse on light ground, but the organic materials are still needed to improve fertility and retain summer moisture.

When to plant Timing is governed by two main factors—the type of plant and the weather. Generally evergreens are best planted in early autumn, although large specimens probably establish more rapidly as growth is starting in April and May. In mild winters, however, or on well-drained light soils, planting can be carried out at any time from late September until May, provided the ground is not waterlogged, frozen or covered with snow.

Deciduous shrubs and trees (those that drop their foliage in autumn) can be put in from leaf-fall until about mid-April but again, this must be delayed in bad weather. Container-grown plants—not to be confused with containerised specimens, which are lifted from the open and potted for sale—can be planted at almost any time. Make sure that they have plenty of moisture if you put them out in summer.

1 If conditions are unsuitable for planting, place shrubs in a sheltered spot and cover bare roots with moistened sacking.

2 Take out a planting hole larger than the root ball. Break up the soil at the bottom of the hole, working in plenty of humus.

3 A length of wood placed across the hole will enable you to check that the plant is set at the correct depth.

4 If a stake is needed, drive it into position before filling in with soil.

5 To get the best effect from a collection of small shrubs, first arrange them in position.

6 Trim off any torn or crushed roots before planting, using sharp secateurs.

7 A screen of fine mesh netting around newly planted evergreens will help to prevent drying out but won't exclude any light.

8 Sprinkle some bonemeal around each shrub at planting time; this slow-acting fertiliser benefits most plants.

Early pruning

Several shrubs can be pruned early, provided that the branches are not frosted, to encourage strong growths on those that flower on the current year's wood or to give a coloured stem display.

1 Large-flowered clematis like Nelly Moser and *Clematis jackmanii* that bloom before mid-June can be pruned. Remove the dead wood and shorten side shoots back to the first pair of buds.

2 Clematis that flower after mid-June can be cut back to a pair of healthy buds about 3ft (90cm) from the ground.

3 Shrubby dogwoods like *Cornus alba,* grown for its stem colour, can be pruned back hard to encourage a crop of new shoots. Leave first-year plants unpruned.

4 Varieties of the half-hardy *Fuchsia magellanica* can be pruned to about 9in (23cm) from the ground. In mild districts where strong bushes are established, cut back to living wood.

5 Check other shrubs for diseased, dead or badly placed branches.

6 Spray deciduous shrubs with a winter tar oil wash to kill any overwintering pests. This is important on spindles (euonymus), which can harbour blackfly.

Get roses into shape

When there is a frost-free day, go over the roses and get them into shape before the main pruning starts. Old, neglected roses will be overcrowded and probably full of dead wood. Removing weeds now will make it easier later on.

1 Collect up and burn all the rose foliage that has accumulated under the bushes over the winter period. This is especially important if the bushes suffered from black spot last year.

2 Where grass and weeds have become entrenched in neglected beds it may be necessary to apply weedkiller from an old watering can to kill or weaken them.

3 If not already done in autumn, reduce the height of bushes to prevent wind rock damage to roots. Remove all hips and dead wood at the same time.

4 Annual weeds can be removed by hand and the soil loosened up by shallow forking over the surface. Don't dig too deeply as this may loosen the bush roots.

5 You can sprinkle a handful of bonemeal around each bush now, but do not use fast-acting fertilisers which would be wasted at this time of year. While cleaning the rose beds, lightly fork in rough peat, compost or rotted manure after applying the bonemeal.

6 Newly-planted roses can be cut back to about 6in (15cm) from the ground. Also prune out any dead stems and tread firm any plants lifted out of the ground by frost.

MARCH
Jobs for March
The earliest shrubs to flower, such as *Mahonia japonica,* and other shrubs can be given a fertiliser dressing.

Detach rooted layers from shrubs and plant in permanent positions.

Many tree and shrub seeds can be sown in a sheltered border of fine soil Some will not germinate the first year, so choose a place where they will not be disturbed. Rub stratified fleshy seeds (see page 141) between your hands to remove the hard seed from the covering.

Ivy growing on walls can be clipped back with a pair of shears. Take off the leaves to expose bare stems, which will soon leaf up again.

Summer flowering heathers
Between the end of April or early May, when the winter heathers have finished flowering and the summer heathers have not yet started to display, there is a gap of only a month. During early June there are three species of merit that will be showing flowers—*Erica cinerea, E. ciliaris* and *E. tetralix.* There are also a few hybrids and the daboecia varieties.

A beautiful sloping heather garden with stone steps

Erica ciliaris **and** *E. ciliaris* **Delta**

Erica cinerea has produced many cultivars, the flowers of which vary from white through various shades of lilac, pink and red to purple. Outstanding ones are C. D. Eason with bright red flowers, Domino, whose white flowers contrast well with its deep green foliage, and P. S. Patrick, a strong grower with rich purple flowers. Of the new forms with coloured foliage, Golden Drop, although not a strong grower, is outstanding, having old gold foliage that turns a fiery red during winter; flowers are lilac, but rather sparse.

Erica ciliaris cultivars are few in number. Although all are attractive with their large racemes of egg-shaped flowers, the branches are brittle and break easily. Those worth growing include Globosa with pink bells, Mrs C. H. Gill, a glowing red, and Stoborough, which has large white flowers.

The cultivars of *Erica tetralix* are ideally suited for wet gardens, thriving in cool, moist soils. But although they will grow in most acid soils they resent dryness at the root. *E. t. alba mollis* is outstanding, not so much for its pearly white flowers but for its new foliage which is shining silver. Of the hybrids, *Erica x watsonii* Dawn is a good garden plant, producing its large pink flowers from late June until September.

All of the summer heathers require an acid soil, a pH of 4.5 being ideal. In gardens where the soil contains free lime it is better to grow them in a raised bed of acid soil.

Winter and spring flowering heathers
Winter flowering heathers are a 'must', giving a cheerful display of colour from December to April, when few other shrubs are in flower. Provided that the soil is in good heart and acidy, but not overdry, they will thrive with a minimum of attention, quickly forming neat clumps. There are a few that are ideal for ground cover and, even when out of flower, the different foliage colours are sufficient to merit their place in the summer garden.

The soil ideally should have a pH of 5.5 which, although not as acid as some of the summer heathers prefer, will grow winter heathers to perfection. On neutral soils of pH 7, if a hole 12in across by 8in deep (30 × 20cm) is taken out and the top 4in (10cm) mixed with the equivalent amount of peat, it will be just right to plant each winter heather.

Every second spring after planting they should be given a tablespoon of Growmore and a teaspoonful of magnesium sulphate. This should then be dressed with 1in (2.5cm) of wet peat or pulverised bark. Under no circumstances should heathers be fed with basically nitrogenous fertilisers—ie, sulphate of ammonia. They would elongate and soften the growth, which leads to frost damage and a short life span.

The dwarf compact growers will rarely need trimming, for the new growth quickly buries the dead flower heads naturally, keeping the plant tidy. The stronger growers may need clipping each year and this should be carried out in late April when the flowers have faded.

APRIL
Jobs for the month

It is dangerous from now on to plant bare-rooted trees or shrubs. Container-grown plants can be put in at any time.

Water is always essential at transplanting time, whatever the weather, and may be needed at intervals all through the coming summer.

Hydrangeas don't need regular pruning but old wood can be cut out now if growth is overcrowded, and if flowers have been small in the past.

Planting evergreen hedges

This is the ideal time for planting evergreen hedges for privacy and protection for the garden. The Leyland cypress is quick-growing, but it may need protection itself in the first season. They should never be allowed to dry out completely at the roots when they are trying to get established.

Winter jasmine, flowering currants and forsythia are best pruned immediately they have finished flowering.

A top dressing of peat between all heathers and worked into the centre of old plants will cause new roots to grow. Rooted pieces can then be taken off and replanted.

Leyland cypress planted as a hedge can be topped now if they have reached the required height.

3 Test plants for correct depth, spacing them 18–24in (45–60cm) apart depending on the height and thickness required. Tall hedges need wider spacing.

1 It's much better to take out a continuous trench for a run of hedge plants, rather than dig individual holes. Make the trench wide enough to take the roots without crowding.

2 Make the trenches deep enough to take the root balls so that the top of the compost is at ground level for container plants. Fork peat into the base of the trench.

4 Add some general balanced fertiliser to give plants a good start and on heavy soil mix sharp sand and peat to the infill soil. Fill in gradually, firming down the soil as you go, so that it is well worked in between the roots of lifted plants. Securely tie each plant to a cane or stake and, if the site is exposed, give some protection from drying winds by erecting a temporary screen of polythene sheet or hessian.

131

MAY
Jobs for the month
Layering is the easiest and safest method for the amateur to increase rhododendrons. Pegging down flexible lower branches into shallow trenches is better practice than mounding over stems pegged at ground level, as the latter tend to dry out more rapidly.

Replacing rosemary
Rosemary is a wonderfully aromatic shrub, which is useful as a herb in the kitchen. Old plants are not worth keeping, so plant new ones now in a sheltered, sunny place or take cuttings to give a batch of youngsters for planting next year.

Shrubs to be pruned immediately after flowering include kerria, berberis and spiraea.

Rhododendrons, azaleas and lilacs should be dead-headed as soon as flowering ends.

3   Ideal shoots are 3–4in (7.5–10cm) long. Trim off the lower leaves and shorten the heel. Cuttings will root in a sandy compost either in pots or direct in the ground under a frame or cloche. A hormone rooting compound speeds things up.

1   If bushes suffered from cold winds last winter, damaged shoots can be trimmed back to living wood, by cutting just above a healthy side shoot.

2   If your plant is now old and straggly, propagate by selecting healthy side shoots of last season's growth for use as cuttings. Remove these with a 'heel' of older wood.

4   Young plants raised from cuttings last autumn should be pinched at the growing tip to encourage a bushy habit. Remove any flowers in the first year to promote leaf growth.

JUNE

Jobs for the month

Climbing plants may need tying in and watering, especially those growing against a wall.

Potted shrubs that had been removed to the greenhouse or conservatory for early flowering should be put into plunge beds outdoors. Avoid exposing them to excessive sun or to strong draughts.

Weather conditions may dry out the soil, so keep newly planted shrubs supplied with water. Encourage next year's display by pruning back shrubs that have finished flowering. Cut back to strong side shoots.

Half-ripened cuttings

From now until autumn you can increase many shrubs by taking cuttings of half-ripened shoots. Hebe (veronica) cuttings will root readily in a cold frame and will give young plants for planting out next year.

3   Dipping the stem into a hormone rooting liquid will hasten striking of your cuttings.

1   Select and remove healthy half-ripened side shoots with a small heel of older wood. Shoots 3–4in (7.5–10cm) long are ideal.

2   Trim off lower leaves and shorten heel of old wood. Long shoots can be trimmed off to a suitable length just under a leaf joint.

4   Insert cuttings into a moist, sandy compost, then place in a cold frame or propagator. Shade from bright sun and spray periodically to stop the compost drying out.

Rose maintainance

Roses will be in full growth by now. Keep them in top health by coming down hard on weeds, pests and other troubles early.

1 Neglected rose beds can be cleared of weeds by using Weedol or Murphy's Rose Bed Weed-killer (soluble). More persistent offenders can be treated with Casoron G.

2 Continue to tie in rambler and climber shoots to keep the plants tidy and easy to maintain. Remove badly placed shoots with secateurs.

3 If you want good, exhibition-type blooms, remove the smaller buds that appear on either side of the large terminal bud. Regular spraying with insecticides and fungicides must continue.

4 In moist conditions, look out for botrytis, which can severely disfigure blooms and prevent buds from opening. Spray with a systemic fungicide.

5 Mildew is another common fungus disease prevalent in moist summers. Prevent it with proprietary rose fungicides or use a systemic to deal with any infections.

JULY
Jobs for the month
Cut again fast-growing hedges such as *Lonicera nitida,* privet and thorns that were trimmed in April. Slower-growing hedges such as hornbeam, beech, holly, and the conifers can receive their first cut.

Wisteria can be pruned this month or next, cutting back side shoots to leave five buds.

Complete the pruning of early summer-flowering shrubs.

Dealing with rose suckers
Suckers are shoots arising from roots below the ground on bush roses, or on the trunks of standard types. Regularly check your roses and remove any suckers before they sap the plant's strength.

Most roses are really two plants joined together by a process known as budding. The roots are a wild rose, the top part a cultivated one. This makes the bush grow stronger. In standard roses the trunk is also part of the wild rose.

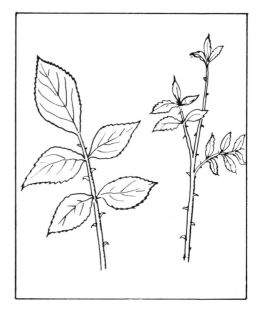

2 Sucker shoots are generally paler green with more thorns and the sprays have seven or more leaves instead of the usual five. Remember, too, that they always come from below ground.

1 Generally, the cultivated rose takes all the plant's energy, but sometimes the wild rose will send up shoots. They always come from below the soil and must be taken off or they will starve the best rose to death.

3 If suckers are just cut off at ground level they grow more strongly than ever. The soil must be scraped away and the whole shoot pulled away from the roots. If they are on the trunk of a standard rose, cut them right back close to the stem.

AUGUST
Jobs for the month
In severe winters, the hardy fuchsias like *F. magellanica* and its varieties can be cut back by frost, so it's as well to take cuttings now to replace any losses. These plants are easy to root—all you need are warm and shady conditions where the compost is not likely to dry out. Take cuttings in the same way as for the other shrubs previously mentioned.

If you want to increase heathers and ericas in quantity, try striking short cuttings this month. This method is not as easy as layering in spring, but is ideal when only one or two parent plants are available. Use basal wood of the current year's growth, reduce cuttings to 1in (2.5cm) long and root round a pot with sharp drainage. Keep shaded and moisten compost by frequent overhead sprays rather than soaking with a can.

Taking rose cuttings
Roses raised from cuttings have the advantage of not producing stock suckers. Many species are readily raised in this fashion, as well as floribunda and hybrid tea types. Choose a cool and sheltered spot where the soil is unlikely to dry out quickly, but the ground must drain well.

1 Select unflowered, semi-ripe shoots and trim off the lower leaves, but leave the small buds at the leaf joints.

2 Trim the heel of older wood carefully or cut under a joint, then dip the base of the cutting into a hormone rooting powder or solution.

Many shrubs will suffer during warm, dry periods, so provide temporary shading wherever possible, give overhead sprays in the evenings and keep the roots well watered. Keep the plants tidy by dead-heading once flowering has finished and tie in new growth.

3 Rose cuttings are treated in a similar way to other hardy shrubs. Choose a sheltered area in the garden, dig over the site and make a V-shape cleft with a spade. Add some sandy compost to aid rooting, then insert the cutting for about half its length. Firm in with your foot.

4 Keep the soil moist and don't worry too much if the upper foliage and stems die back, as the cutting can break out from the buds at the base of the stem.

Opposite

Above left Centaurea montana (cornflower) can be sown direct in March or April. *Above right* Phlox comes in annual and perennial forms, both of which are easily grown. *Below left* Cotinus coggygria (the smoke tree) is a bushy shrub, which gets its name from the spreading hairs that give a smokey effect. *Below right* Cistus skanbergii is a form of rock rose that likes a well-drained, limy soil and a sunny spot in the rock garden.

SEPTEMBER
Jobs for the month

The hardy fuchsia cuttings inserted last month may have produced a root system and require potting into small pots or plastic cups with drainage holes. Overwinter them in a cold frame or sheltered spot outside.

Shrub cuttings of half-ripe wood can still be taken and rooted in a frame, and layered cuttings can be pegged down to root.

Give fast-growing hedges their final trim and clip evergreen hedges again.

Watch for mildew on all types of shrubs and spray where necessary.

Rambler roses should be pruned, cutting out the flowered canes and tying in this season's new ones to replace them.

Taking a camellia cutting

Camellias are expensive shrubs to buy, so try taking leaf/bud cuttings this month. Use only lime-free compost.

1 Take a healthy shoot of current year's wood and cut up into 1in (2.5cm) lengths. Each section should bear a leaf and live bud.

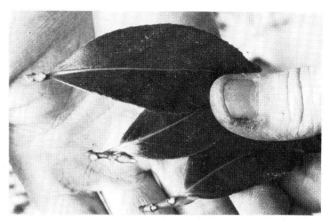

2 The terminal part of shoots can be trimmed off just under a leaf joint, or lower stem sections can be sliced lengthways to reduce the thickness by a half.

3 Insert three or four cuttings treated with a rooting powder into a 3½in (9cm) pot of moist, lime-free compost or equal parts lime-free sand and moss peat. Buds should not be completely buried.

4 It's very important not to allow the cuttings to dry out, so place the pot in a closed propagator frame or seal it in a clear polythene bag and keep it shaded.

Opposite

Above Tagetes or French marigolds are superb bedding annuals that are best raised under glass in March and planted out in late May or early June. *Below* Many different species of tulip are available; bulbs should be planted out in autumn for flowering the following spring.

139

OCTOBER

Jobs for the month

Preparations can begin now on sites for new shrubs and trees to be planted next month.

Take hardy shrub cuttings of fully ripened wood. As these large, fully developed shoots will root overwinter, this is an ideal method of growing a hedge from scratch. Use a hormone rooting compound and strike under the protection of a cloche or cold frame.

Clearing up fallen leaves is a never-ending task, but one that must be undertaken periodically, especially on rockeries. Pile healthy leaves into a corner to rot down, but burn any from diseased plants.

Potting hebe cuttings

Hebe (veronica) cuttings struck earlier in the year should have established root systems by now. Unless the weather has turned hard, they can be potted individually and over-wintered in a cold frame ready for spring planting.

1   Gently knock out the cuttings from their pots and if a good root ball is apparent, prepare to pot them on. If the root ball is dry, water and allow to drain.

2   Separate the cuttings' root systems by hand, being careful not to damage the finer hair roots.

3   Each plant will need only a small pot, up to 3in (7.5cm), well-crocked and filled with compost.

4   Gently firm compost down round the roots so that the surface is level and about $\frac{1}{4}$in (6cm) below the rim of the pot. Pinch out growth to encourage bushiness.

5   Overwinter the young plants in a cold frame positioned in good light, as these plants are evergreen and will make a little growth during mild spells.

NOVEMBER

Jobs for the month

Take any hardwood cuttings of shrubs that you haven't got round to yet.

Prune climbing roses and finish pruning ramblers.

If hybrid tea roses are pruned back severely now they are unlikely to suffer wind-rock through the winter.

Rose hips can be gathered if you want to try growing from seed. They should be stratified.

All deciduous hedges can be cut back.

This is the main month for planting trees and shrubs lifted from the open ground.

Shrubs that you wish to force into early flowering in the greenhouse can be potted and plunged into a sunny, sheltered place outside until moved under glass in December or January.

Stratifying seeds

Tree and shrub seeds will germinate more easily when you sow them next spring if they are stratified. This process helps to break down the tough seed coat and consists of removing seeds from the fleshy berries, etc, then storing them in moist sand or compost in a cold place over winter.

2 Soft pulpy berries can be crushed, using a rolling action on those containing a tough-coated seed (hawthorn). Rose hips and similar can be cut open to extract seeds.

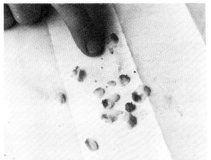

3 Where possible, remove seeds from the pulp—allowing the flesh to dry out a little will make the job easier. The myrtle berries shown have fairly small seeds.

4 A few cleaned seeds can be placed in tins after mixing with moist, sandy compost—they're then ready for sowing. Large numbers of seeds are placed in alternate layers of moist sand in large containers.

1 Harvest berries or hips as soon as they are fully ripe or immediately they drop off the tree.

DECEMBER
Jobs for the month
High winds can be very troublesome at this time of year. Partially prune back rose shoots now and check that the plants are supported by stout stakes or trellises and secured by reliable ties.

Clematis jackmanii can be pruned from any time between now and February (see page 128).

Continue pruning roses if not already finished.
Trees need overhauling too
Cavities, snags and broken branches are all potential trouble spots on trees and shrubs. Clean up these danger points now. To prevent cavities refilling with water, drill through to the lowest point to provide a drain hole, then cement up when the weather improves.

3 It's essential to protect the wound against further infections, so apply one or more coats of tree paint or a bitumen wound dressing containing fungicide. Heavy snow or high winds will soon find any weaknesses. Here a crotch has split because of rot and torn the bark. Remove the branch carefully and treat the wound as already directed.

1 Remove all snags left by bad pruning or branches breaking off in wind. Saw off flush with the main branch, first making an undercut if the snag is a long one.

2 Where fungus infection has got into main branches, remove as much rotten wood as possible with a chisel and mallet. Then smooth off wound edges with a sharp knife.

4 Where branches cross over, rubbing will damage bark and could result in disease. Prune out all crossing branches and thin out overcrowded shoots. Ensure litter is not allowed to accumulate in cavities or branch crotches. This large cavity needs filling with cement next summer, after the walls have been treated with bitumen.

Lawns

JOBS FOR SPRING

April and September are the months for sowing grass seed. For a new lawn, sow at the rate of 1–2oz per sq yd (28–57gm per sq m).

Where grass is thin on older lawns, scratch the surface and sow at $\frac{1}{2}$oz per sq yd (15gm per sq m).

Moss killer should be applied before raking moss out. Bare patches left will need seeding or turfing.

Apply spring fertilisers according to the manufacturer's instructions. Distribute evenly and water if rain does not come after 24 hours.

Make sure that edges are straight by putting down a line and cutting with a half-moon spade.

Hormone weedkiller is best applied when weeds are growing fast. The first application can go on now. Be sure to wash out the can thoroughly afterwards, or better still, use a separate can. Dispose of mowings away from the garden for two or three weeks afterwards.

Worm casts should be brushed off before mowing or the edge will be taken off the blades. Several wormkillers are available if the trouble is too bad.

Where the lawn edge is broken down by treading or a wheelbarrow, cut the turf about 1ft (30cm) back into the lawn, turn it round with the firm edge on the outside, fill the hole with soil and sprinkle with seed.

Apart from watering and mowing there are a number of other routine tasks to carry out in spring if you want your lawn to stay in tip-top condition.

Spring-cleaning

Spring is a good time to get rid of any dead grass and to apply a top dressing of lawn peat. This will add humus to the soil and improve its water-holding capacity.

Rake out dead grass and moss with a lawn rake. After spiking, spread the top dressing evenly over the lawn. Brush peat into the holes made by spiking.

Spiking

Before watering, go over the whole lawn with a spiker or garden fork making holes at least 6in (15cm) deep and 6in apart. This will allow the water to penetrate right down to where it's needed—the roots.

Fertilising

All lawns will look better if they are fed with proprietary lawn foods during the growing season. Fertiliser can be applied with a spreader or by hand.

Filling in bare patches

After the early season clean-up, the lawn may well show some bare patches where weeds previously grew, Re-sowing these with seed will soon restore your turf to its original glory. Keep it neat by maintaining a clean edge.

2 Where bare patches have appeared, break up the ground and add sieved soil to fill up holes where large weeds have been removed. Rake down level.

3 Re-sow bare patches, preferably with the same grass mixture, or any hard-wearing mix on turfed lawns. Large patches need $1\frac{1}{2}$–2oz per sq yd (45–60gm per sq m). Keep them moist and protect seed from birds by covering the area with crossing cottons.

1 If a few persistent weeds like dandelions have resisted the application of a lawn weedkiller, cut them out individually with an old knife or treat with a spot weeder.

4 Where grass has grown into the border and the edges are looking ragged, use an edging iron to cut neat, clean lines. A board is useful for maintaining straight edges.

Sowing a new lawn

The cheapest way to obtain a lawn is without doubt from seed. The best time to do this is in the spring, when there is a good chance of both rain and warmth to germinate the seeds. Summer sowing is possible, except in the middle of a heatwave, but regular watering with a sprinkler is essential

1 Dig over the ground, removing weeds and roughly levelling at the same time. Spare soil is used to fill dips. Spread a layer of lawn peat about 2in (5cm) thick over the whole area.

2 Work the peat into the top few inches of soil and then roughly level the whole area with the back of a fork. Firm the soil by systematic treading.

3 Apply a base dressing of lawn fertiliser. Rake the area level. Note that the head of the rake is held almost horizontally to the soil.

4 The best way to ensure that the seed is evenly distributed is to use a lawn spreader. If you are sowing by hand, mark out the area into square yards or metres.

5 Distribute one handful of seed evenly one way across the marked area, and another in the other direction. After sowing, the seed should be lightly raked into the surface. String up as many noisy, shiny bird scarers as possible to protect the seed.

JOBS FOR SUMMER

To keep a good lawn through spring and summer it must be continually growing and continually mown. If either of these stops, the turf quickly deteriorates. July and August are the critical months when you really have to work at keeping a lawn presentable, especially during any periods of hot drought.

Feeding

The best time to apply food is in spring and autumn. Summer feeding should be regarded more as a supplement or boost. The main need is nitrogen, and this, applied in conjunction with enough water, will keep a lawn growing and green. It must not, however, be used after the end of August.

Sulphate of ammonia is the cheapest and best nitrogenous fertiliser for grass, but if relied on entirely it could build up trouble. However, if balanced fetilisers or manures containing phosphates and potash are used in spring and autumn, $\frac{1}{2}$oz of sulphate of ammonia to 1 sq yd (15gm per sq m) three or four times during July and August will do nothing but good.

The best way to apply it is just before, or even during, a rainstorm, or after a soaking with the hose, and giving a drop more water just to dissolve it and wash it in. Don't put it on dry or it will blacken the grass.

Mowing

This does not just mean cutting and taking away excess growth. It has a great effect on the lawn's quality and general well-being. Two things are essential: a machine that cuts well and its timely and careful use.

Usually, because of the weather, there is less grass to take away in July and August than at any other time in the cutting season. But this doesn't mean that mowing should be less frequent. The mower should be used as often, even if sometimes there is little grass removed.

For a time in the spring, hard close mowing induces new growth, but in mid-summer it can be damaging, particularly if the ground is dry. It is best to raise the blades gradually to leave the grass longer and thicker.

Make sure at this time too, that the machine is razor-sharp and properly adjusted. Don't neglect the edging of the lawn. Clean edges contribute more to the appearance of a garden than any other single factor.

Weeding

Summer neglect could well lead to an invason of weeds. Moss and weeds will continue growing in conditions that will slow down or stop grass, and they will soon gain a strong hold. Unfortunately midsummer is not the best time for weed-killing and the best treatment is to keep the grass growing.

The odd dandelion or plantain can be spot treated with weedkiller, or removed with a knife, but the selective hormone killers are best used in May and June.

One of the worst lawn weeds, strangely enough, is a grass itself—the annual meadow grass. This dies in the winter and leaves bare patches. One of the dangers of mowing without collecting the clippings is that the many seeds of this grass are spread. For that reason alone, always mow with the box on when annual grasses are ripe.

Watering

It takes a lot of water to make grass grow and a hosepipe is essential, preferably with a sprinkler attachment for even distribution. Just damping the top intermittently with a watering can will encourage short roots near the surface and hot, dry days will still cause trouble. The aim must be to saturate the ground to a depth of several inches.

Turf and mower maintenance

The lawn, like the rest of the garden, needs regular attention during the summer. Cut regularly, making sure that the mower blades are sharp, and water thoroughly in times of drought. Remember that grass makes an ideal material for composting if mixed with other types of material, or it can be used immediately as a light mulch round shrubs and other crops.

3 If your mower is not cutting cleanly, check to see if the blades are sharp. This rotary blade has had a rough time cutting grass on stony soil and needs re-sharpening.

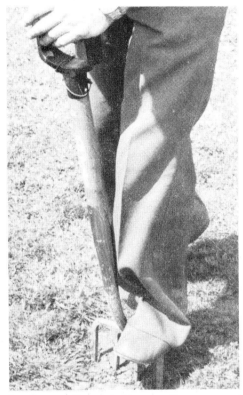

1 On well-used lawns the ground may get compacted and harden up during dry spells, so it's advisable to spike. Push the fork or aerator tines down for their whole depth.

4 During hot, dry weather, set mower blades to give a high cut. Give frequent light cuts during summer, leaving off the grass box. Large rotary machines may need a side-thrower attachment.

2 Grassed areas will suffer from drought, so give lawns a good soaking periodically. Oscillating lawn sprinklers or spray lines give good coverage.

5 Clean off compacted grass clippings after using the mower, but to avoid accidents always disconnect the plug or leads from the machine before exposing the blades.

Keeping on the level
If the mower appears to miss patches of grass or tends to scalp areas, there is probably some unevenness in the lawn level. Provided the affected area is small you can easily rectify the trouble with some prompt lawn 'surgery'.

3   Remove surplus soil from bumps or add a well-drained soil mix to hollows, raising turf to the correct level.

1   Using a board as a straight-edge, make an H-shaped incision in each area of the lawn where there is a bump or hollow. An edging tool is best for this job.

4   Replace the soil flaps and check the level, then tamp back firmly with a wooden tamper or the back of the spade.

2   Carefully insert a spade into the cross-piece of the incision and undercut the turf so that it can be rolled back in two flaps without breaking up.

5   Fill any remaining cracks with a compost mix or peaty soil, and keep the area supplied with water during any dry spells.

148

JOBS FOR AUTUMN
Tidying up
As long as the ground is not frosted you can get on with tidying up the lawn before winter sets in. Rake off any fallen leaves before mowing.

If left, fallen leaves will cause yellow patches and worms will drag them into their burrows, so rake them off periodically. Burn any twiggy debris. During mild spells the grass will continue to grow, so keep it cut, but with the mower blades set fairly high.

If you didn't get a chance to scarify the lawn in spring, now's your chance to remove dead grass, thatch and weeds. This will help avoid fungus infections. Spiking helps drainage and aeration if the ground is heavy.

On badly-drained soils, brush in sand, then apply an autumn lawn feed at the rate recommended on the bag. Granular types can be applied by special spreader—use a flower pot for the dust types.

Turfing a lawn
Autumn is the best time to lay a lawn from turf, although this job can be done at any time provided that the ground is not frozen and that an adequate water supply is at hand. Make sure that you get good quality turf and insist on seeing it before buying so that you can check that: (1) it is weed-free; (2) it has a high proportion of fine grasses; (3) it has plenty of fibre at the base; and (4) it is evenly cut to the same depth. Prepare the site in the same way as for seeding, but the tilth need not be so fine. You will need a flat-tined garden rake, a knife and enough boards to reach across the area.

1   Start by laying the first row, making sure that it will finish about 1in (2.5cm) above the level of any adjoining paving.

2   At the ends of the first row lay the end turves lengthwise to the proposed finishing line. Pull the turves into each other with the back of the rake.

3   Use the knife to cut the last crossways turf into the lengthways ones to obtain good joints.

4   Put the boards on the first crossways row and lay the next row. Pull this into the last with the back of the rake. Some people bond the turves like brickwork, but it is not really necessary.

5   Tamp the newly laid turf down with the rake to maintain an even level. When you've finished, put the sprinkler on it to keep it continually wet. Allowing the new turf to dry out would cause it to shrink and cracks would appear between the pieces. Don't walk on the turf for at least a fortnight. After a few weeks it will benefit from a light rolling.

JOBS FOR WINTER
Overhaul the mower

Winter is the best time to overhaul and clean all mowers and safeguard against rust by using rust preventer or oil.

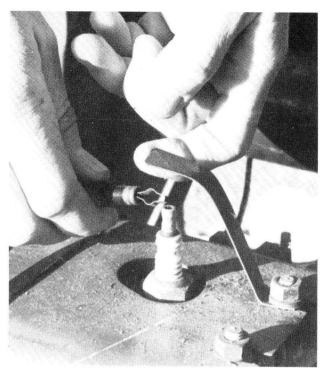

1 Before starting work, take the precaution of disconnecting power leads to engine. This goes for petrol or electric machines, including battery ones.

2 Thoroughly remove all dirt and compacted debris. If left it will hold moisture and encourage rust.

3 Wire wool or a wire brush should be used to remove flaky rust. Once it has been cleared, apply one of the many rust removers/preventers to protect bare metal.

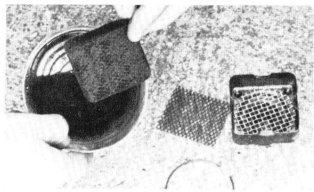

4 Check air filters on petrol engines and clean by washing in petrol.

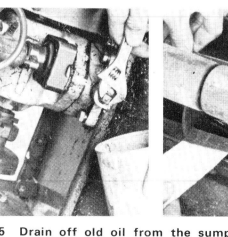

5 Drain off old oil from the sump if power is by a four-stroke petrol engine. Replace with grade of oil recommended in maintenance handbook. Test sharpness of cylinder mower blades by placing a piece of paper between blades and back plate. If they don't cut cleanly, have them resharpened.

Greenhouses and frames

FINDING THE BEST SITE

The perfect place for a greenhouse rarely occurs naturally in the small garden, so we have to make do with the best one available. Let's try to put site requirements into some kind of order of importance:

1 First the business of full light. Be very wary about any place where the whole of the house doesn't get maximum light.
2 Next the drainage. If you can, avoid a wet, badly drained spot. Water may lie about and will be a problem. Such places are also particularly cold and dank in winter and are more expensive to heat and keep dry.
3 Then the accessibility. In fine spring and summer weather, a walk to the greenhouse at the top of the garden might be considered a real pleasure—but there are times in winter when it would almost certainly be cursed.
4 The question of connecting the mains services, water, gas or electricity, may well come into the reckoning, so what about a site close to supply lines?

Now we come to the compromises that will almost certainly have to be made. Regarding the light, buildings and/or trees to the north or east, for instance, can help to provide shelter from cold winds. As long as the light from the south is uninterrupted, they can almost be considered an asset.

A lean-to greenhouse is ideal on a south-facing wall. They are always more naturally warm if they are in this position.

Even if there is a tree or similar to the south, some obstruction of strong sunlight from that direction from mid-day to around 3pm is acceptable.

Next we come to drainage. Steps that can usually be taken include draining the site or raising the greenhouse on to a concrete floor. Plants of all descriptions can then be grown on staging, or in the modern way, on the floor in growing bags.

The question of getting to and from the greenhouse is more of a personal decision. How far will you want to walk on cold nights to check heating and cover cold frames? How much trouble will it be to open and close ventilators perhaps two or three times a day? These things have to be done, whether it's two yards or two hundred.

Finally something that is worried about too much by the beginner . . . should the house run north to south or east to west? Really it hardly matters. With most amateur houses there is not much difference between length and width anyway.

What is more important, if it's possible to do it, is to avoid having the door facing due north or east. A cold wind driving in every time it is opened can put up the heating cost considerably in a small house.

CHOOSING A GREENHOUSE

In recent years the range of greenhouse designs has increased enormously. The tried and tested traditional designs are, however, probably the best bet for most gardens where a general collection of crops and pot plants is required, but the more unusual modern ones are ideal for awkward positions, such as the patio or on a large balcony if you live in a flat.

If we take a look at the more traditional shapes we find there are two main types—the full-span house and the half-span or lean-to, which is, in fact, a span house cut down the centre of its length.

The full-span house has vertical side walls and an apex roof. The pitch of the roof will vary from one model to another, but be sure it's steep enough to clear itself of snow. An important variant of this type is the Dutch-light house, which has side walls that slope outwards. When sited correctly the Dutch-light house makes maximum use of sunlight, particularly during winter. This is a useful feature if you want to grow crops in the ground—lettuce for instance—during the period when the sun is low in the sky and the cost of heating is high.

Taking light-catching construction even further is the Hartley range of houses, which have angled glazing bars running from the ridge to the side walls. This feature is also incorporated into their lean-to models, which are ideal for siting against a south or south-west facing wall.

The lean-to type of house is an advantage if space is at a premium, but it also has the benefit of the back wall acting like a storage radiator, thus holding the heat longer during the night.

Recently there has been a trend towards the mini-greenhouse, and there are several lean-to designs that could be useful if your garden is small or if you are perhaps restricted to a balcony. As you would expect, the growing area is limited and you cannot walk into such structures, but there is normally sufficient room to house a growing bag or two for tomatoes and shelving space to raise all the bedding plants a flat dweller could hope to cultivate.

Many people are building a patio into their garden, so it is not surprising that the greenhouse manufacturers have come up with some new designs with this in mind. Of the types available several have a near-circular base wall plan and are formed by multi-sided units in wood or metal.

Most of such 'circular' houses have definite side wall and roof sections, but the geodesic Solardome is unique in having no such distinctions. It is made from numerous triangular panes of glass, arranged to form an igloo-like structure.

With the introduction of clear plastics into greenhouses, the true curve has made its appearance. Many firms now offer walk-through tunnel houses, most of which feature a rounded roof, but others have an apex roof and distinctive side walls, although the angles of ridge and eaves are rounded off to prevent the cladding material from tearing.

JANUARY
Jobs for the month
Without heat Bring inside bowls and pots of bulbs for early flowering, also pots, tubs, etc, of shrubs for forcing into flower.

With heat Make sure extra heating arrangements are ready for an early start next month. Soil warming cables can be laid out ready.

Bring chrysanth stools inside; watch for greenfly and leaf miner.

Carefully take off any dead or dying leaves from primulas, cinerarias, calceolarias, cyclamen, etc.

Hardy spring-flowering shrubs like camellias can be gently forced into bloom now. Given a temperature of 45–50°F(7–10°C) and plenty of ventilation on mild days, these will give colour during February and early March in the greenhouse or even on a house windowsill.

Time to start tomatoes
Sow tomato seed towards the end of the month in heat for planting in the greenhouse where an early crop is required. For a main crop under glass, or for a cold house planting in spring, delay sowing until next month. The seedlings can be raised either in the greenhouse (heated) or a warm room of the house.

Planting lilies
For an exotic, fragrant show in the greenhouse during summer, lilies are a good choice. Little is required in the way of heat, but sharp drainage is essential. Although some are lime-haters, most standard composts are perfectly safe.

Crock a clean clay or plastic pot with broken pieces of pot or large pebbles. Single bulbs will need a 6–7in (15–18cm) pot, and several bulbs a larger container. Cover the crocks with a layer of rough peat or fibre to prevent compost blocking the drainage hole, then partially fill the pot with a John Innes or peat/sand potting compost. Lily bulbs should be firm and have a good root system. Check the base for signs of rotting and remove damaged scales. Treat small areas of rot with fungicide dust.

Stem-rooting lilies like *Lilium regale, L. speciosum* and *L. auratum* are planted about two-thirds down the container. Those varieties with basal roots go about half-way. Pots containing basal rooting lilies are filled to 1in (2.5cm) below rim. Stem rooting kinds are only just covered and pots are topped up gradually as shoots grow. Compost should be moistened at planting, but no more water is required until growth starts. Keep frost-free until shoots appear, then maintain a temperature of 45–55°F (7–13°C).

3 It is not too difficult to get seedlings to this stage if they are kept at around 65°F (18°C). They will be like this about two weeks after sowing. This is the stage when they are best moved on into pots or boxes.

1 If the seeds are spaced out about $\frac{1}{4}$in (6mm) apart there is less tendency for them to be drawn up tall in the early stages. Pushing them individually off a piece of glass is an easy way of keeping them separate.

2 Harbinger is an old variety but, because it ripens quickly, it is particularly suitable for early sowing.

4 The aim is to grow short, sturdy plants like this for planting out. Only in good conditions of light and warmth will such plants be produced.

Increasing early chrysanth stocks

Chrysanthemums under glass will need regular attention, particularly where stools are under cold frames. Where heat can be provided, you can take cuttings.

1   When weather conditions are mild, open up frames that are overwintering chrysanth stools. This will prevent a muggy atmosphere, which soon leads to disease problems.

2   Go over the stools and check for signs of grey mould fungus and pests like aphids. Spray or dust the new shoots with suitable control.

3   If you have a heated greenhouse or propagating frame, early chrysanths can be raised by stool cuttings. For preference, select shoots growing from the stool roots.

4   Trim the shoots down to 2–3in (5–7.5cm), making a clean cut just under the leaf joint with a sharp knife or razor blade. Remove one or two of the lower leaves.

5   Rooting mediums should be good quality John Innes compost or a well-drained peat type. Cuttings can be dipped in a hormone rooting dust or solution before insertion. Place the pots in a greenhouse or propagating frame where a minimum temperature of 50°F (10°C) can be maintained. Keep the compost just moist.

FEBRUARY
Jobs for the month
Without heat Start watering chrysanth stools to produce cuttings.

Bring seed sowing composts inside, have pots, boxes, etc, ready to start.

Sow lettuces, broad beans, peas and brassicas, all for planting outside later, in frames or cloches. Also sow beetroot, carrots, spring lettuces, salad onions, radishes, peas and early potatoes directly where they are to mature and protect with cloches.

With heat Sow seeds of all early vegetables for transplanting outside later, and half-hardy bedding subjects. Keep at 55°F (13°C) minimum.

Take cuttings of chrysanths, geraniums, fuchsias, etc, as they become available.

Box up dahlia and begonia tubers to provide cuttings, if not already done.

Sow tomatoes and cucumbers in warmest spot.

Pinch out tips of schizanthus plants.

Sow begonias, mixing the dust-like seed with fine dry silver sand to enable you to sow thinly and evenly. Do not cover.

The economics of frames and cloches
Frames and cloches will repay their cost and earn their keep, in a shorter time than anything else you can buy in the garden. Cloches bought in early February for instance could make this year's lettuce a month earlier, protect your strawberries from the birds and give you outdoor tomatoes to pick in July instead of August—your money back in less than six months.

A frame installed will do the same, and if you are starting crops in a warmed greenhouse, a frame is a necessary addition anyway, to provide a 'half-way house' for plants raised inside to become used to being outside.

Both cloches and frames will pay for themselves if they do nothing but this spring work. But there are other crops that they can be used for at other times to give you the real bonus.

Frames, of course, can be heated quite easily with electric cables. Then they become almost as useful as the small warm greenhouse. But it must be remembered that if you have a heated frame, you still need a cold one too. The move from one temperature to another must always be gradual and in easy stages.

Do-it-yourself cloche clips for holding glass or plastic sheet together are offered by several different firms, providing a means of using spare and waste pieces of either material.

Ventilating, protecting and watering frames
These considerations are of the utmost importance, as neglecting them could easily kill or seriously harm plants. The amount of air admitted depends on the types of plants and the time of year. Young plants and seedlings, which should make quick growth, need a warm, moist atmosphere; overwintering plants like some air on all

A cold frame is invaluable for raising early plants for sowing outside later on

favourable occasions to encourage sturdy growth; flowers in bloom prefer a dry atmosphere.

Any plants will suffer from violent temperature changes so, on a potentially warm spring day, open the lights a little in the morning, increasing ventilation progressively as the sun gains power. During a settled period of warm spring weather lights can be taken off completely in the middle of the day, and in summer dispensed with altogether, depending on the crop in the frame. To capture what heat the sun has had during a bright winter or early spring day, completely close down the gap in the lights in mid-afternoon. When severe frost threatens, cover the frame with mats, old overcoats or any other handy protective material.

Plants need most water in spring and summer, so water at least once, and preferably twice, each day. In winter one water a week is generally adequate. Summer watering should be done in the morning or evening, not in the height of the sun, but in spring, late autumn and winter, stick to mornings only, as excessive night-time moisture would probably cause the fatal condition of 'damping-off' of plants.

Opposite
Clematis — a favourite climber with different varieties available to flower from late spring through to early autumn. This lovely bloom is growing through a camellia bush, hence the different foliage.

Vegetables under cloches from mid-February onwards

Crop	Method
Aubergines	Obtain plants for setting mid- to late May; uncover end of June
Beans, broad	Sow direct mid-February; uncover at the end of March
Beans, dwarf	Sow direct end of March; uncover in June
Beans, runner	Sow in pots or box at the end of April for planting outside in mid-June
Beetroot	Sow direct end of February; uncover early April
Brussel sprouts, cabbages and cauliflowers	Sow in short drills mid-February; uncover at end of March for transplanting outside in April
Capsicum (peppers)	Obtain plants for setting mid to late May; uncover end of June
Carrots	Sow direct mid-February; uncover early April
Cucumbers (outdoor)	As capsicum, or sow seeds direct mid-May
Lettuce, spring	Obtain plants for setting in March; sow seeds direct mid-February; uncover in May
Lettuce, winter	Sow direct in August/September; cover in October/November
Marrows	Obtain plants for setting mid-May or sow seeds direct in early May; uncover mid-June
Melons	Obtain plants for setting in early June; keep covered
Onions, spring salad	Sow direct mid-February; uncover early April. Cloches also useful for ripening bulb onions after lifting
Parsley	Sow direct in March; uncover early May; replace in October for winter picking
Peas	Sow direct mid-February; uncover early April
Potatoes	Plant direct mid-February; protect cloche in frosty weather
Radishes	Sow direct mid-February; uncover late March
Strawberries	Cover plants end of February until picking ends
Sweet corn	Obtain plants for settings mid to late May; uncover end of June
Tomatoes	As sweet corn; cloches can also be placed over plants in September to assist ripening

Cloches can also be used for hardening off plants raised in a warm greenhouse although they do not give as much protection from the cold as a cold frame.

Opposite

Above left Webbs Wonderful — a legendary cabbage lettuce, which, though slow growing, has many large crisp leaves. *Above right* Tight-headed varieties of summer cabbage are superb chopped up in salads. *Below left* Melons grow well in Britain provided that they are given the protection of a frame or large cloche. *Below right* Who says that vegetables aren't attractive? These two rows of well-grown cabbages are a handsome sight.

Dwarf beans under the protection of an Essex cloche with sliding panels for access

Vegetables in cold frames from mid-February onwards

Crop	Method
Aubergines	Obtain plants in May for growing in frame through the summer, uncovering when they reach the top light
Beans, broad	Sow in pots or boxes mid-February for setting out at the end of March
Beans, dwarf	Sow in pots or boxes mid-April for setting out mid-May
Beans, runner	Sow in pots or boxes end of April for setting out early June
Brussel sprouts cabbages and cauliflower	Sow in mid-February for setting out in April
Capsicum (peppers)	Obtain plants in May for growing in frame through the summer, uncovering when they reach the top light
Cucumbers (frame)	As above, but lights are kept on throughout growth; shade from sun
Lettuce	Sow mid-February for setting outside in early April
Melons	As for cucumbers, but plant two weeks later
Marrows	Sow in pots early May for setting outside mid-June
Onions	Useful for ripening bulbs after lifting
Peas	Sow in mid-February in pots or boxes for setting outside end of March
Tomatoes	As aubergines

Bedding plants can be raised from March seed sowings, or boxes of plants can be obtained and kept until planting out time.

Chrysanth and fuchsia roots can be kept through the winter and cuttings taken from them in April

Dahlia tubers can be started into growth in April.

Sweet peas can be started in October or February.

Cuttings of shrubs, trees and perennials can be put in the frame in mid and late summer.

Where a frame is on a depth of garden soil, dwarf beans, capsicums, cucumbers, aubergines, lettuce, melons and tomatoes can be planted direct into it. Otherwise they must be in suitable pots and boxes.

If a cold frame is used in conjunction with a heated frame or greenhouse, the seedlings or plants are transferred at the time indicated for obtaining plants in the tables on page 157.

Repot fuchsias

If you have a heated greenhouse or warm room indoors you can tidy up potted fuchsias and repot them ready for producing new shoots in a few weeks' time.

1   Give the root ball a good soaking by immersing it in a bucket for about half an hour. Watering a dry root ball with the can will not have the desired effect. Trim back the side growths to get the plant into shape, but don't be too drastic as the final pruning can be done later in spring, when the shoots start growing.

2   After the root ball has been allowed to drain, carefully tease away the outer part of the old compost, taking care not to damage the roots.

3   Repot into a clean pot of the same size or one slightly smaller. Use fresh John Innes or peat compost and gently work this down firm with a rammer so that no air spaces remain.

4   Finally give the leafless plant an overhead spray with tepid water. The addition of a systemic fungicide will discourage fungus diseases. Place in a warm room or greenhouse.

MARCH
Jobs for the month
Without heat Sow for transplanting outside later early vegetable seeds of lettuces, cabbage, cauliflowers, onions, leeks, etc.

Start watering old fuchsias to produce cuttings.

Bring potted strawberries inside.

With heat Sow seeds as for last month, also *Primula obconica* and coleus for pot plants.

Take cuttings of dahlias and chrysanths.

Prick out and pot on all seedlings when big enough to handle.

Hardiest subjects can go into the cold frame to make more room.

Pot on all decorative pot plants where necessary.

Ventilate during warm days.

Potting lily-of-the-valley
Few scents can rival that of lilies-of-the-valley. By potting up at intervals through the year, a succession of flowers can be achieved. Lifted roots can be forced during winter and early spring, and retarded crowns can be used at other times.

3 Work the compost between the roots, but do not firm hard. Cover the roots with loose compost, but leave tips of crowns showing above surface.

4 If the crowns are wanted for pot decoration, plant the roots vertically; again they can be planted closely together. Cover the tips with a thick layer of moss until the shoots are developed.

1 Lift established crowns from the garden now, or buy the special retarded ones for a succession of bloom. Reduce the root length to make potting or boxing easier.

2 Where cut flowers are required, lay the crowns in closely packed ranks in shallow boxes of light, peaty compost or fibre, with the roots at an angle for convenience.

5 Keep the moss and compost moist, place in a cold frame for about four days, then take into a heated greenhouse or propagating frame to force at 55–60°F (13–16°C).

Pot flamboyant hippeastrums

Hippeastrums (often called amaryllis) are one of the most flamboyant plants for the home or greenhouse. Potted now and started at a temperature of 60°F (16°C) they will produce enormous trumpets in late spring or early summer.

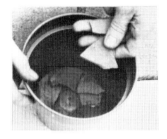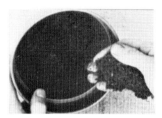

1 Hippeastrums may remain in the same pot for up to four years, so good drainage is important. Cover the holes at the base of the pot with a layer of stones or broken pot. Cover the crocks with some rough material like coarse peat, which will stop the compost from washing down to the bottom of the pot and clogging the holes.

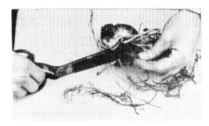

2 The biggest bulbs usually give the best show of blooms, but choose only undamaged ones that are firm and support a reasonable root system. Remove dead or shrivelled roots.

3 Add well-drained compost—like J.I. No. 3 or a sand/peat mixture—firming this between the roots. Fill the pot to within $\frac{1}{2}$in (13mm) of the rim. Note that only two-thirds of the bulb is buried. Put in a stake now to avoid damaging the developing root later on.

Taking dahlia cuttings

If you plunged over-wintered dahlia tubers in good compost a few weeks ago, there should now be plenty of cuttings ready for taking. First prepare small pots or trays of the rooting mixture, which can be almost anything. Best results will be obtained in a small propagating box, but rooting can be achieved on the open bench, although the new cuttings will have to be shaded from strong sunlight. Ensure a night temperature of at least 60°F (16°C).

Remove the cuttings from the tubers with a sharp knife or blade, selecting ones about 3–4in (7.5–10cm) long, and trim them just below a node (the point where the leaf joins the main stem). Take a cut fractionally above the 'eye', as this will allow further cuttings to develop that can be taken later on.

Although the dahlia will root readily, use one of the many rooting powders to be absolutely sure. Insert each cutting firmly into the pots or trays. Each small pot will take five or six, and a tray will hold 40 or so comfortably.

For the first day or two the cuttings may flag. A light spray with warm water each evening will soon revive them. It takes about 14 days for a dahlia cutting to develop roots—somewhat longer with a few varieties.

It is now urgent that you provide them with a home of their own. The first potting should be in a 3in or $3\frac{1}{2}$in (7.5cm or 9cm) pot. Then, later in the spring, towards planting time, they can be moved into larger containers.

1 Prepare cuttings for rooting by trimming them just below the lowest pair of leaves. A rooting powder may be used.

2 A $3\frac{1}{2}$in (9cm) pot will comfortably hold five or six cuttings. On the right is a pot of cuttings rooted successfully, which takes about 14 days.

APRIL
Jobs for the month
Without heat There is still time to sow many of the quicker-growing half hardy annuals for bedding out in June.

Sow outdoor cucumbers and marrows.

Plant tomatoes at the end of the month.

Most cuttings root easily at this time of year. Fuchsias, geraniums, coleus and chrysanths will all make useful plants from small shoots set in a small pot of peat/sand mix, covered with a polythene bag.

Chrysanths in cold frames should have the lights taken off completely on fine days. Cover again at night and protect with matting or similar if frosts are forecast.

Bedding plants hardening off in frames need ventilation during the day. Prop lights up with a flower pot, but guard against cold winds blowing in.

Early vegetables in frames may be attacked by slugs. A few slug pellets scattered around are a good insurance.

With heat Tomatoes and cucumbers, peppers and aubergines can be planted.

Move all early bedding subjects and vegetable plants, as well as geraniums and fuchsias for planting outside, into the cold frame.

Sow marrows, courgettes, celery, French beans and outdoor tomatoes.

Plants just pricked out or potted on need shade from strong sun. Danger time is from noon to 3 pm. A sheet of newspaper fixed in the right spot will do the job.

Quick-growing bedding plants that can still be sown include marigolds, alyssum, nemesia and zinnias.

Sow indoor varieties of tomatoes and cucumbers where they can be kept warm at night. Harden off during May and plant in early June.

Knocking a cucumber plant out of its pot to be potted on into the growing container

Earlier sown bedders will be ready for pricking out into boxes. Allow 2in (5cm) between plants, water in with a fine rose on the can and shade for a day or two.

The tops can be pinched out of tall-growing geraniums to make them bush out. There is still time to take and root cuttings, which will make flowering plants by June. Pinch out tips of dahlias and fuchsias as well.

The earliest planted tomatoes will be in flower. A fine spray of water directed up into the open flowers will help them set fruit. Feed as soon as fruits start to swell.

The first side shoots taken from tomato plants can be rooted as cuttings and will make plants that will grow outside.

Leaf cuttings

Cape primroses (streptocarpus) grown from seed often give good colour forms that are worth increasing. To do this you can divide up the plants, or for greater numbers, propagate by leaf cuttings, which root without much trouble.

1   Select only healthy, strong-growing leaves, if possible taking only those that will not unbalance the shape of the plant.

2   Cut up the leaves into 2–3in (5–7.5cm) sections by drawing a razor blade cleanly across the leaf blade. It is important that each segment has a portion of the main vein.

3   Apart from the lower segment holding the leaf stalk, trim off the bases of each to form a V-shape, which makes insertion into the compost easier. Rooting powder will speed growth.

4   Insert the cuttings into crocked pans of a peat/sand mix or a John Innes seed compost in ranks and gently firm in with the fingers. Give the pot a good soaking and allow to drain.

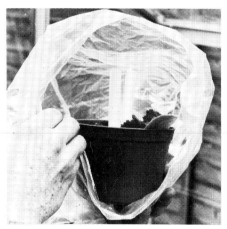

5   Place in a warm propagator frame or cover with a clear polythene bag to retain humidity. Segments will quickly root and produce plantlets at 60–65°F (16–18°C).

MAY
Jobs for the month
Without heat Sow tomato and runner bean seeds for planting outside in June.

Box dahlia and begonia tubers to start into growth, if not already done.

Pot up all rooted cuttings and prick out seedlings.

Shade may be necessary on sunny days. Attend carefully to ventilation. Avoid leaving water lying around at night.

With heat Sow runner beans for planting out in June, also cinerarias, calceolarias and primulas for next spring flowering.

Pot on begonias to be grown outside.

Water and feed hydrangeas copiously.

Feed tomatoes at least twice a week when two or more trusses are set.

Shade cucumbers and spray regularly with clear water.

Planting tomatoes in an unheated greenhouse
One of the month's first jobs in an unheated greenhouse is to put tomato plants in their fruiting stations. They can go into a sterilised bed, growing bags or rings, the last two methods being best if your previous crops have been affected by disease or soil pests. Whalehide rings are widely available but you can also make your own from felt or old lino.

Whether you take out the existing bed soil or make up a raised bed, put down a layer of heavy gauge polythene sheeting to isolate the aggregate from the soil. Make some slits through the polythene to provide drainage, then fill in the trench or trough with an aggregate like granite chips, coarse sand or gravel to a depth of about 6in (15cm).

Rings 9in (23cm) wide are spaced 20–24in (51–60cm) apart on the aggregate and filled to within 2in (5cm) of the top with a John Innes No. 2 or peat compost. Allow the aggregate and compost to warm up for a couple of days before planting. Insert cane supports as you plant to avoid damaging the roots later. During the early stages of growth all watering should be into the rings. This also applies to any feeding necessary. As first flowers open, aggregate can be damped down.

Re-pot tuberous begonias
If late-started tuberous begonias for bedding out have produced a good root and shoot system they can be moved from their boxes of moist peat into 5in (12cm) or larger pots to grow on. These plants don't like hard potting and should be shaded from hot sun. Good drainage is important, with a peaty compost, not firmed down too hard.

1 Use a well-drained, peaty compost, taking care not to firm it down too hard.

2 Pot the tubers when growth is well developed, taking care not to damage shoots or roots when lifting from the trays.

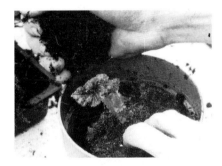

3 Fill up with more compost so that the tuber is just under the surface. Exposed tubers that are concave (basin-like) will tend to collect water and could rot. Gently firm down the compost and keep it just moist by spraying until the roots are established and foliage grows away, then apply plenty of water.

Geranium stem cuttings

Build up a stock of your favourite geraniums (pelargoniums) by taking stem cuttings from healthy plants now. The compost should be moist at first, but until growth gets under way apply only enough water to keep it from drying out.

1 Select healthy, firm shoots from mature plants that show plenty of growth. Cuttings can be taken from all types of geraniums.

2 Trim off the lower leaves and cut the stem just under a leaf joint. If large quantities are taken, sterilise the cutting tool after each batch.

3 Dipping the stems in a hormone rooting compound can assist more rapid root formation. Insert the cuttings into pots of well-drained compost, singly into small plastic drinking cups or in groups in larger containers.

4 They will soon root in a heated greenhouse or propagating frame, where the temperature can be maintained at 55°F (13°C).

JUNE
Jobs for the month
Without heat See that tomatoes, cucumbers, etc, are well supported. Spray tomato flowers with water around mid-day to help setting. Start to feed when fruit swells.

Pot on geraniums, fuchsias and all decorative pot plants.

Take hydrangea cuttings.

When leaves of established grape vines are well developed, pinch back laterals to two leaves beyond a fruit truss. In the first year of fruiting, however, pinch back to just beyond the first truss, as more than one bunch of grapes to each lateral tends to weaken growth. Then in following years, allow a maximum of two or three trusses. Once the grapes start to swell, cut out any small, overcrowded fruits in the centre of each bunch.

With heat Where tomatoes, etc are filling the house, many plants can be removed to the cold frame after it has been cleared of bedding subjects. In this category are azaleas, hydrangeas, Christmas cactus, cyclamen and pelargoniums.

Light shade over the glass will reduce the need to water.

Seeds of cinerarias, calceolarias, *Primula malacoides* and *P. obconica* not sown last month can be sown now and will produce flowering pot plants for a display from late winter into spring. Once the seedlings form two true leaves, they should be pricked off into boxes, spaced 1in (2.5cm) apart, and then into 3in (7.5cm) pots as the leaves touch.

Care of tomatoes
There are several different methods of supporting greenhouse tomatoes. If they are in growing bags, you can use wires and soft twine; otherwise use canes and twine. Keep the plants growing healthily by controlling pests and maintain their vigour by feeding.

2 Tie the other end of the twine to a support wire stretched across the roof. Allow extra twine for running up to the roof to support further growth.

3 Gently twist tomato shoots round the twine, taking care not to damage foliage or flower trusses. Remove the sideshoots as soon as they are large enough to rub out easily. Left to develop they rob the plant of energy that should be used for growth by the leading shoots.

1 If you don't have a growing bag support, fix plastic-covered wire along the tops of the bags and tie soft garden twine to this at the base of the plants.

JULY

Jobs for the month

Without heat When the lower leaves of grape vines on side shoots growing from the laterals are well formed, pinch the shoots back to one leaf from the lateral. Fruit of some varieties may start ripening towards the end of the month. During this time, ventilate if the temperature rises above 70–75°F (21–24°C). Stop feeding the vines when the grapes start to change colour.

The calceolarias, primulas and cinerarias sown last month will be at the pricking out stage when two true leaves have developed. Get them into boxes or small pots as soon as possible.

Regularly side-shoot tomatoes and take male flowers off cucumbers.

Provide shade, plenty of ventilation and damp down regularly to increase humidity.

Watch for pests building up—whitefly, etc—and tackle them at first signs.

With heat Pinch tops out of tomatoes if they are to be cleared in September for late chrysanths.

Leaf section cuttings of streptocarpus started in early April will have produced a batch of plantlets ready for potting on to give flowering plants next summer. Don't discard healthy old leaves as, re-inserted, they will often give a further crop of plantlets.

Coleus provide wonderful plants for foliage decoration, the brilliant colouration of the leaves living up to its name of Flame Nettle. Try increasing stocks of particularly good ones by stem cuttings made from strong side shoots. Cuttings need to be $2\frac{1}{2}$–3in (6.5–7.5cm) long and will root, several round the edge of a pot, in a shaded place. If there are signs of flower buds at the tips, nip them out to direct energy into making new growth.

Begonia rex leaf cuttings

Just a single healthy leaf of the beautiful Begonia rex will provide numerous new foliage plants to brighten your greenhouse and windowsill.

1 Select a healthy, mature leaf and remove from the parent plant by cutting as near to the base as possible to avoid rot setting in.

2 Crock a shallow pan or tray and fill to within $\frac{1}{4}$in (6mm) of the rim with peaty compost. Press the leaf, underside downwards, into the compost, gently but firmly.

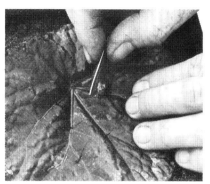

3 Sever the main veins with a sharp blade at regular intervals over the surface.

4 Make sure the severed portions make contact with the compost by holding them down with pebbles or securing with a hairpin. Place the tray in a warm propagator frame or polythene bag to root. Plantlets will develop at the points the veins were cut.

Coping with high temperatures

High temperatures in the greenhouse will pose the major problems at this time, so make sure the house is adequately ventilated and shaded. Where capillary or other forms of auto-watering devices are not installed, damp down daily to reduce loss of water from the plants.

1 Check each morning to see if plants need water and damp down staging to provide cool, moist air around the plants. Avoid wetting foliage of tender plants in hot, sunny conditions.

3 Remove all dead or fading flowers and foliage promptly as they provide a home for many pests and diseases, which romp away in the warm, moist atmosphere.

2 Damping down the floor will also create a humid atmosphere. It also deters greenhouse red spider mite.

4 Encourage a free flow of air and help keep temperatures steady by ventilating as much as possible. A closed house will be more liable to diseases. Ensure that staging is adequate too.

AUGUST

Jobs for the month

Without heat Pinch out tops of tomatoes, but continue side-shooting and feeding.

Take cuttings of geraniums and regal pelargoniums.

Pot on rooted hydrangeas.

Plant freesia bulbs six in a 5in (12cm) pot.

Start watering old cyclamen corms for taking into the house later.

With heat Tomato leaves can be taken off from around all fully developed fruits to assist ripening.

Cut cucumbers while young.

Sow seeds of schizanthus for April flowering, also cyclamen and freesias.

Pot cinerarias, etc, on into final pots.

The coleus cuttings inserted at the begining of last month should now be well rooted and ready for potting up. Don't leave the job too long or the roots will get badly entangled and you'll break them when separating the plants.

One of the most popular flowers indoors during the colder months is the cyclamen. Sown now, the plants will be ready for flowering from the late autumn of the following year onwards. They require little artifical heat during winter, but insist on good light and drainage conditions.

Keep winter cherries growing

Winter cherry plants make a fine show during the dark months through to spring. Seedlings from a late spring sowing will need potting on to avoid suffering a check.

2 These late spring sown plants, pricked off into plastic cups, are ready for repotting. Don't allow them to get rootbound or they will be slow to re-establish in new pots.

3 Repot into $3\frac{1}{2}$–4in (9–10cm) pots. Allow at least $\frac{1}{4}$in (6mm) space at the top of the pot for watering.

1 Aphids are attracted to winter cherry plants, especially the soft growing tips, so keep a watch for these pests and spray with an insecticide such as malathion.

4 To encourage bushy growth, force the laterals into growth by pinching out the growing tips. Established plants will need a weekly liquid feed.

Greenhouse cucumbers

An important point to remember with greenhouse cucumbers is to keep the plants growing as long as possible in warm and moist conditions. Unless you have the all-female types, keep removing the male flowers to prevent bitter fruits.

1 Remove all male flowers to prevent pollination of the female blooms. Males are easily recognised by the lack of an embryo fruit behind the flower.

2 Also remove tendrils to direct the plant's energy into making more growth and encourage fruit production.

3 Fruits are borne on the side shoots (laterals); pinch these out two leaves above a developing cucumber to allow a sub-lateral (secondary side shoot) to grow away for further fruit production.

4 When the leading shoots reach the required height, remove the growing point.

5 Keep cucumbers well supplied with moisture and feed each week with a liquid fertiliser. To get maximum cropping, let the plants grow for as long as possible.

SEPTEMBER
Jobs for the month
Without heat Seeds of several annuals can be sown now, for flowering early next spring. Cornflower, nemesia, godetia, antirrhinums, etc, will live through the winter if kept fairly dry.

Chrysanths must be brought inside towards the end of the month after thoroughly spraying with insecticide.

With heat Clear tomatoes, clean and fumigate greenhouse and bring inside the earliest budded late chrysanths.

At first signs of bad weather also bring in pot plants from cold frames, watching for slugs and other pests, and have heating equipment ready.

Sow short-day lettuce.

Provided enough heat can be given to keep out winter frosts, poor man's orchid (schizanthus) is an ideal annual for sowing now to give a magnificent greenhouse display early next spring. There's usually plenty of seed per packet, so keep a little in reserve for sowing next spring to provide bedding material.

Economical heating
Full greenhouse heating all the year round has become a luxury that few of us can afford. To maintain 60°F (16°C) throughout the whole house in December, January and February is a costly business, whatever kind of fuel and heating equipment are used and however small the house. But make no mistake, it is well worthwhile to provide some heat.

The most economical way for a fair return is to provide enough heat—38–40°F (3–4°C) minimum—to keep things from freezing during the worst months. And then have supplementary local heat—50–60°F (10–16°C)—in a small space, to get seeds and cuttings started in February or early March. This can be done with a soil warming cable or bench, a propagator or a propagating frame.

Alternatively, a small area can be screened off with polythene, and the main heating apparatus or a small paraffin or electric heater used. The extra heat is necessary for six to eight weeks if started in February. By the end of March the natural temperatures are increasing and less warmth will do. By the middle of April, or thereabouts, even this can be done without.

The time it is needed again at the end of the year depends, of course, on the season and the crops grown. But towards the end of September it generally becomes necessary. October to February, then, heat enough to maintain 38°F (3°C), February to early April, a small area to hold 55–60°F (13–16°C), finishing with the ordinary heating for about a month. This programme will keep and grow most of the seeds, plants and crops the ordinary gardener wants.

A lot can, of course, be done with an entirely cold greenhouse. The most important thing is to realise its limitations. There is a great temptation to start things too early, especially when the weather seems favourable, or to attempt plants that are not suitable. The trouble is that failures cost money and bring disappointments. It's far better to keep well within the limits our climate lays down.

Forcing wallflowers
There's no need for your greenhouse to remain almost empty in winter because you can't afford to heat it. Try potting up the best of the most forward wallflowers into 6in (15cm) pots of compost for scent and colour from Christmas onwards. Put the pots in a cold frame to establish and then bring back into the greenhouse to bud.

1   Choose only compact and busy plants for potting up. Lift carefully with a trowel, retaining as much of the root system as possible.

2   Crock a 6in (15cm) pot, add J.I. or peat potting compost, and place the plant so that the top of the soil ball rests ¾in (2cm) below the rim to allow for watering. Well firm the compost using a wooden rammer, especially where a light peat type is used. Make sure that no air spaces remain round the soil ball. Give the plant a good soaking and allow it to drain off before housing it in a cold frame that receives plenty of light. Pots are moved to the greenhouse in bud.

OCTOBER

Jobs for the month

Without heat Pick all tomatoes and take inside for ripening.

Keep the atmosphere dry as chrysanths open, watering them carefully.

Remove geraniums and other non-hardy plants into warmer quarters.

Plant bulbs of tulips, daffodils, hyacinths, etc, for early flowering.

With heat Remove any shading from glass, although chrysanth blooms can be shaded to delay opening.

Give begonias in pots less watering and stop feeding.

Use the greenhouse if possible to dry lifted dahlia tubers, gladioli corms and begonias.

Pot up some fibrous rooted begonias lifted from outdoor beds.

Tuberous begonias will be dying back now, so prepare them for storage by removing all foliage and stems. Dry out the root ball and store the pots on their sides, or remove all the soil and store the tubers in dry peat or sand in a dry place at about 50°F (10°C).

By boxing up the underground stems of mint every three weeks or so, you can get a succession of tender shoots from now until next May. Choose strong plants that are free from rust disease (symptoms are blackish, powdery spots in autumn) and force in a warm sheltered frame or greenhouse.

Overwintering pelargoniums

Pelargoniums (geraniums) still in the open will be in serious danger of frost damage, so if there are any you want to keep for propagating next year, lift and take them indoors after checking for pests and disease.

2 Remove damaged or dead foliage and faded flower heads. Buds can be left to give an extended display indoors if required.

3 Remove most of the garden soil and look out for signs of underground pests such as cutworms. Use a well-drained compost and pot larger plants separately.

1 Lift only the healthiest and best forms for overwintering in a frost-free greenhouse or sunroom. Burn any showing symptoms of disease like rust or virus.

4 Tie in shoots of large plants to keep them tidy. Batches of small plants can be boxed up. Clear off pests by spraying with malathion or systemic insecticide.

An autumn clean and overhaul

Once the last of the summer crops have been cleared, make sure that the structure gets a thorough overhaul. Check for broken glass or deteriorating putty that could allow draughts and heat loss. Also ensure that the heating system is working efficiently and clear the inside of the house of pests and diseases by washing down with disinfectant.

1 If temporary liquid shading has been used during summer, wipe if off with a moist cloth or sponge to allow maximum light penetration in winter.

3 Give the inside of the greenhouse a thorough wash down with a disinfectant. A sprayer is ideal for getting into awkward places like extruded metal framework. Also wash down the staging and floors. It may be best to remove all the plants at this time. Hose clean capillary bench matting, sand or gravel used on benches.

2 Check glazing clips or putty and renew them if necessary to prevent draughts and heat loss during the colder months. Replace any broken glass immediately. Clear away any crops that have finished. Check all foliage for pests and diseases before adding them to the compost heap, and burn any suspect material.

4 Conserve heat by putting up polythene sheet insulation. Fix to wooden houses by stapling, or bolt on to metal models using a card washer to prevent tearing.

NOVEMBER
Jobs for the month
Without heat Cut down chrysanths to around 9in (23cm) and give little water when blooming is finished.

Clear out tomatoes, cucumbers, etc.

Generally clean up greenhouse and fumigate. A sulphur candle can be used if house is completely empty.

For freesias early next year pot up some corms 2in (5cm) deep in well-drained compost and water sparingly until growth shows.

With heat Bring inside pots of bulbs for Christmas flowering, and plant others.

Gradually reduce the water supply to geraniums, both cuttings and older plants.

Potted azaleas will need more water than anything else, and also feeding as soon as flower buds show.

Water Christmas chrysanths carefully and stop feeding.

Transplant lettuce.

If you can maintain a minimum temperature of 45–50°F (7–10°C) you can grow the early flowering gladioli over winter for an early spring show in pots. Plant five corms in each 5in (12cm) pot and cover with compost to about 1in (2.5cm). Try species like *Gladiolus colvillei* and varieties like Peach Blossom or Spitfire.

Overwinter early chrysanth stools
If you want to propagate further stocks of early chrysanths, lift and move the stools into the protection of a cold frame or greenhouse. Shoots produced from the stools can then be used as cuttings next year.

1 Cut down the stems of early varieties to within 9–12in (23–30cm) of the ground. To lift stools from the open ground, push the fork in about 6in (15cm) from the stems on three sides, then ease it out on the fourth. Cut down any existing basal shoots to ground level.

2 Small quantities of stools can be washed in water containing a little disinfectant. Otherwise just remove surface soil to get rid of algae and weeds.

3 Trim off any coarse roots and either pot or box up stools using a well-drained compost.

4 Give a thorough watering and move into a frame or greenhouse. Further watering should not be required until next month. Dust stools with BHC powder and add slug pellets.

DECEMBER
Jobs for the month
Without heat Carry out repairs and painting where necessary, if not already done.

Cineraria care
Cinerarias should be growing away strongly with a few showing buds early in the month. Keep the compost just moist and give budded plants a weak feed, but avoid splashing water on the foliage. Encourage good air circulation.

With heat Cut down chrysanths after flowering and, if room is needed, tip out of pots and pack together in boxes.

Bring more bulbs inside.

Prune vines back to two buds from source of side shoots.

Bring rhubarb roots inside for forcing either this month or next, also seakale and chicory.

Make preparations for early sowing next month.

1 Closely set pots will produce spindly growth and dangerous humidity around the leaves, so space them out to allow air and light.

3 Aphids and leaf miners are likely to appear, so apply a preventive control regularly. Insecticidal dusts are preferable at this time of year.

2 Remove all traces of dead or fading stems and foliage promptly or fungal infections are sure to result.

4 Cinerarias need only a minimum of heat, so ventilate the house on mild, sunny days. If gas or paraffin heaters are used, always allow a little ventilation.

Pests and diseases

Problem	Description	Effect	Treatment
APPLE SAWFLY Grubs attack in June; not to be confused with codling moth, whose grubs attack in July and August	Young grubs leave a sticky mess on the outside of fruitlet where they enter, then burrow just under the skin, leaving a ribbon-like scar; the maggot leaves the fruit through another hole in July	Appearance is spoiled at very least, and attacked apples may drop off when quite young	Spray trees with BHC or systemic insecticide when most of the petals have fallen; timing is critical
APPLE SCAB Common and serious disease of all apples	Small black spots appear on young fruits, spreading into blackened areas that often crack; brown spots appear on the leaves	General disfiguration of fruit, sometimes spreading to young shoots of trees	Apply lime sulphur or systemic fungicide sprays at regular intervals starting at green blossom bud stage, again at pink bud stage, at petal-fall and often again three weeks after that
BLACK SPOT A common fungus disease of roses	Starts in spring as black specks on leaves that increase in size and become more noticeable in mid and late summer	Leaves drop prematurely in bad attacks; severely weakens bush	Gather up and burn all affected leaves; spray with tar-oil wash in winter to kill spores, and at 14-day intervals through spring and summer with systemic fungicide or collodial copper
CABBAGE ROOT FLY All brassicas are liable to attack, particularly in April and May, but can go on all summer; the eggs are laid just below soil around plant	Maggots eat and damage main root	Plants wilt and turn blue; badly attacked ones shrivel and die, most often in hot, dry weather	Dust seed beds with calomel dust, also apply round newly set out plants; use soil insecticides in the same way
CARROT FLY Fly which lays eggs in May around carrots, just under the soil surface	Damage is caused by small maggots, which bore into roots	Seedlings wilt and die; a sign of attack is reddening leaves. Also attacks parsnips, parsley and celery	Apply soil insecticides before sowing and among the sides of the rows in April and May
CLUB-ROOT A fungus that attacks all the brassica family and can live for several years in the ground	Roots become distorted and swollen often splitting and rotting to give offensive smell	Plants stunted and dwarfed yet usually manage to keep alive	Apply dressing of lime to sweeten sour soil; pay attention to crop rotation, dress seed beds with calomel dust and sprinkle in holes where plants are going
CODLING MOTH The grub is found in the centre of mature apples as opposed to the sawfly maggot which drops out of the fruit in summer	Generally enters the fruit in or near the eye and tunnels to the core	Fruit often drops just before ripening and will not keep	Tie sacking or corrugated cardboard bands round the trunks in July to trap the hibernating caterpillars (remove and burn these during the winter); spray fruits with Fentro in July

Problem	Description	Effect	Treatment
FLEA BEETLE Serious pest of all brassica family, doing most damage on young plants	Small flea-like creatures that attack seed beds, making holes in young leaves during sunny spells in April and May	Checks growth and may completely destroy patches of seedlings	Dust rows of seedlings as they appear with derris and repeat until plants are 2–3in (5–7.5cm) high
GREEN CAPSID BUG Attacks many plants, but particularly fruit trees and bushes, chrysanths, dahlias, roses and beans	Rather like big greenfly but do not congregate in great numbers; first attacks show as spots on leaves, which turn into holes as the leaves grow	Growing plants are deformed, and damaged; young leaves turn brown and stop growing	Apply derris or malathion dust to the tips of shoots during May and June
GREENFLY Most common plant pest, attacks almost all plants but is one of the most easily controlled	Green winged and wingless insects congregate in great numbers in flowers or near growing tips of plants	Weakening and distortion of plants and shoots tending to spread virus diseases from affected to clean plants	Spray with various insecticides at intervals through spring and summer; use systemic insecticides, fumigation of frames and greenhouses
LEAF MINER Attacks weeds that act as hosts as well as cultivated plants	Fly punctures leaves to lay eggs, which become tunnelling maggots; white spots are the first signs, followed by distinctive trails	Weakening of plant and dropping of leaves in bad attacks	Hand pick maggots in slight attacks; spray with malathion or nicotine
LEATHERJACKETS The larvae of the daddy-long-legs feed on all kind of roots	Tough-skinned, legless and about an inch long; because eggs are laid among grass, they are a bad pest where lawns and fields are newly dug	Growth of all plants is affected as roots are eaten	Apply sevin or BHC dust mixed with sand from October to April
MEALY BUG Infests trees, shrubs, greenhouse plants, vines and cacti	Grey insects in cracks and joints of plants, often covered with a white, mealy substance	Loss of vigour, yellowing and loss of leaves in severe attacks	Forcibly spray with malathion or malathion dust
MILDEW Affects many plants but most commonly recognised on roses	Starts as grey spots on young leaves and quickly spreads over all the new growth	Growth retarded and flowering checked	Spray at intervals from April onwards with a rose mildew specific
PARSNIP CANKER Brown patches start around soil level and spread	Enters the roots through cracks or damage done by pests	Bad attacks can make parsnips unusable	Grow resistant varieties and use soil insecticides to deter attacks of carrot fly, which can start the disease
RASPBERRY BEETLE Attacks the fruit of raspberries, blackberries and loganberries	Generally only recognised by the small grubs that are found when picking the fruit	Damages the fruit	Spray or dust fruit trusses with derris middle and end of June for raspberrries and loganberries, early and mid-July for blackberries

Problem	Description	Effect	Treatment
SCALE INSECTS There are many types but damage is similar in all cases; they attack all shrubs and trees and various greenhouse plants	Non-active, remaining firmly attached in one place on twigs, branches, under leaves; looks like small shells	Loss of vigour to the plants; some species produce a honeydew on which black sooty mould develops	Spray dormant deciduous trees and shrubs with tar oil wash, otherwise use a systemic insecticide
SLUGS Will damage all kinds of plants by feeding on leaves, stem and roots; particularly bad in wet, poorly drained soils	Mainly two types: keeled slugs, which feed on underground parts, and field slugs, which eat leaves and stems	Damage or complete destruction throughout the whole garden	Use slug pellets or liquid wherever attacks may occur
TOMATO LEAF MOULD Most common on indoor tomatoes, generally appearing in June	Attacks older leaves first, appearing as pale patches on upper surfaces and later as brown or purple patches on lower leaves; can shrivel leaves completely	Flowers are sometimes affected, but main trouble is general weakening effect	Grow resistant strains; provide adequate ventilation, pick off and burn affected leaves, and spray with systemic fungicide
VINE WEEVIL Larvae and adults attack many kinds of plants, both inside and outside, including cyclamen, cinerarias, begonias, ferns in pots, and rhododendrons, alpines, strawberries and raspberries	Larvae are fat, legless grubs, creamy white with large head; adults, which feed at night, are black, $\frac{1}{2}$in long, covered with short hairs	Larvae attack roots and underground stems while adults feed on leaves at night; root attacks will cause wilting, leaf attacks weaken and disfigure	Dust or spray with insecticides; repot plants attacked into fresh compost or use soil insecticides
WHITEFLY Pest of greenhouse plants and brassicas in the open garden	Small, white, moth-like insects, which congregate on the undersides of leaves and fly up in swarms when disturbed	General weakening of plants, also leaving a sticky substance on which moulds grow	Make repeated sprayings of whitefly insecticide at intervals of 7–10 days to catch hatching eggs
WOOD LICE Generally found where rubbish collects, particularly in greenhouses	Oval, $\frac{1}{2}$in-long dark grey insects with legs and feelers, which roll up into a ball when touched	Will gnaw at all parts of plants, eating holes in leaves	Avoid accumulating rubbish and dust frequented places with derris or BHC dust
WOOLY APHIS A pest mainly of apple trees but will also affect ornamental trees and shrubs, also known as American blight	Insects on shoots and branches are covered with a white, wool-like substance	Shoots become swollen and distorted and general vigour is decreased	Wash dormant trees with tar oil and forcibly apply insecticides during growing season; paint small patches with a brush

Index

179